VIETNAM TRAVEL GUIDE 2023

The Most Up-to-Date Pocket Guide to Discovering Hidden Gems and Planning an Unforgettable Trip to Vietnam

JOURNEY MAVEN

Copyright © 2023 by [Journey Maven], All Rights Reserved. Without the owner's express written consent, no portion of this book may be duplicated, saved in a database, or transmitted by any technology, including electronic, mechanical, photocopying, recording, or other methods.

TABLE OF CONTENT

VIETNAM'S LOCATION IN THE WORLD MAP

INTRODUCTION

INTERESTING FACT ABOUT VIETNAM

BRIEF HISTORY OF VIETNAM

CHAPTER 1
TRIP PLANNING TO VIETNAM

1.1 When To Travel To Vietnam
1.1.1 Map Showing When to Travel to Most Attractive Destinations in Vietnam
1.2 Journey To Vietnam

1.2.1 Journeying to Vietnam from Cambodia

1.2.2 Journeying to Vietnam from Laos

1.2.3 Getting to Vietnam from China

1.3 Entry Requirements and Visa

1.3.1 Passport

1.3.2 Visa

1.3.3 Visa exemptions

1.3.4 Visa-on-arrival

1.3.5 Visa extension

1.4 Currency and Budgeting

1.5 Health and Safety Considerations

1.6 Travel Insurance

CHAPTER 2
THE REGIONS AND CITIES IN VIETNAM

2.1 Red River Delta Region

2.2 Northeast Region

2.3 Northwest Region

2.4 North Central Coast Region
2.5 South Central Coast Region
2.6 Central Highlands Region
2.7 Southeast Region
2.8 Mekong River Delta Region

CHAPTER 3
TOP CITIES ACCOMMODATION OPTIONS FOR TOURISTS IN VIETNAM

3.1 Top Hotels for Tourists in Hanoi City
3.1.1 The Sofitel Legend Metropole Hanoi
3.1.2 The Oriental Jade Hotel
3.1.3 Apricot Hotel
3.1.4 La Siesta Diamond Hotel & Spa
3.1.5 Hotel de l'Opera Hanoi - MGallery

3.2 Top Hotels for Tourists in Ho Chi Minh City (Saigon)
3.2.1 The Reverie Saigon
3.2.2 Park Hyatt Saigon
3.2.3 Caravelle Saigon
3.2.4 Hotel Majestic Saigon
3.2.5 Sheraton Saigon Hotel & Towers

3.3 Top Hotels for Tourists in Da Nang City
3.3.1 InterContinental Danang Sun Peninsula Resort
3.3.2 Fusion Maia Da Nang
3.3.3 Vinpearl Luxury Da Nang
3.3.4 Furama Resort Danang
3.3.5 Naman Retreat

3.4 Top Hotels for Tourists in Nha Trang
3.4.1 Six Senses Ninh Van Bay
3.4.2 Vinpearl Luxury Nha Trang

3.4.3 Mia Resort Nha Trang
3.4.4.Amiana Resort and Villas
3.4.5 InterContinental Nha Trang

CHAPTER 4
MEANS OF TRANSPORTATION IN
VIETNAM

4.1 Getting Around in Cities
4.2 Intercity Transit in Vietnam
4.3 Motorbike rentals
4.4 Taxis and ride-sharing services

CHAPTER 5
VIETNAM FOODS AND DRINKS

5.1 Vietnamese Cuisine
5.2 Street Food
5.3 Traditional Vietnamese Dishes
5.4 Beverages

CHAPTER 6
ATTRACTIONS AND CULTURAL
SITES ACTIVITIES IN VIETNAM

6.1 Historical and Cultural Sites
6.1.1 Ho Chi Minh Mausoleum in Hanoi
6.1.2 Hue Imperial City
6.1.3 My Son Sanctuary in Hoi An
6.1.4 Cu Chi Tunnels in Ho Chi Minh City
6.1.5 Temple of Literature in Hanoi
6.2 Natural Wonders & Scenic Spots
6.2.1 Halong Bay
6.2.2 Phong Nha-Ke Bang National Park
6.2.3 Sapa Rice Terraces
6.2.4 Mekong Delta
6.2.5 Da Lat Flower Fields
6.3 Adventure and Outdoor Activities
6.3.1 Trekking in Sapa
6.3.2 Water Sports in Nha Trang

6.3.3 Motorbiking through the Hai Van Pass
6.3.4 Caving in Phong Nha-Ke Bang National Park
6.3.5 Rock climbing at Cat Ba Island
6.4 Shopping and Markets in Vietnam
6.4.1 Ben Thanh Market in Ho Chi Minh City
6.4.2 Dong Xuan Market in Hanoi
6.4.3 Hoi An Night Market
6.4.4 Saigon Square in Ho Chi Minh City
6.4.5 Hang Gai Street in Hanoi
6.5 Nightlife and Entertainment
6.5.1 Bui Vien Walking Street in Ho Chi Minh City
6.5.2 Hanoi Opera House
6.5.3 Rooftop Bars in Ho Chi Minh City
6.5.4 Nightclubs in Hanoi
6.5.5 Water Puppet Shows in Hanoi

CHAPTER 7
PROVEN & PRACTICAL TIPS FOR TRAVELING IN VIETNAM

7.1 Language
7.2 Etiquette and Customs
7.3 Tipping
7.4 Bargaining
7.5 Using Technology and the Internet
7.6 Staying Safe and Health

CONCLUSION

VIETNAM'S LOCATION IN THE WORLD MAP

Vietnam is situated in Southeast Asia, bounded by the South China Sea to the east, Cambodia to the southwest, Laos to the northwest, and China to the north.

Its exact geographical coordinates are somewhere between 8.4° and 23.4° north latitude and 102° and 109° east longitude.

To offer a more specific explanation, Vietnam is located on the eastern side of the Indochinese Peninsula, stretching over 1,650 kilometres (1,025 miles) from north to south.

Its coastline spans around 3,260 kilometres (2,025 miles), making it the easternmost nation on the Indochinese Peninsula.

Vietnam's land area encompasses around 331,210 square kilometres (127,881 square miles), making it the 65th biggest nation in the world.

The nation is marked by numerous physical characteristics, including a lengthy coastline with magnificent beaches, rich river deltas, mountains, and lush woods.

In the north, Vietnam shares a border with China along the rugged parts of the Annamite Range and the border river system.

To the west, it borders Laos, delineated by the Annamite Mountains. The southern boundary with Cambodia is formed by the Mekong River and its tributaries.

With its strategic position in Southeast Asia, Vietnam acts as a gateway between the Indian Ocean and the Pacific Ocean, making it a vital commercial route.

Its position also adds to the country's diversified environment, with a tropical monsoon climate dominating in the south and a more moderate temperature in the north.

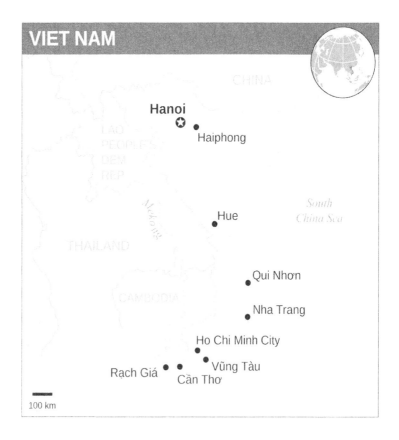

The biggest city in Vietnam is Ho Chi Minh City (previously known as Saigon). It is the economic, cultural, and commercial centre of the nation.

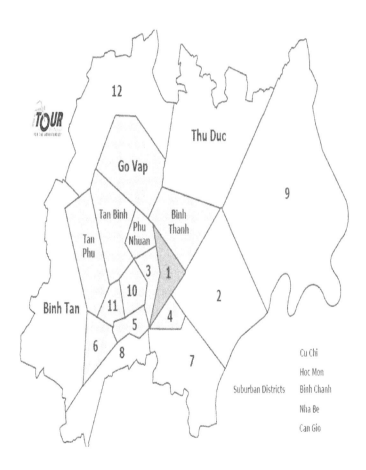

Ho Chi Minh City is situated in southern Vietnam.

The second-largest city in Vietnam is Hanoi. Hanoi is the capital city of Vietnam and is situated in the northern region of the nation. It serves as the political, cultural, and economic hub of Vietnam.

The third-largest city in Vietnam is Hai Phong. Hai Phong is a large port city situated in the northern region of the nation, roughly 100 kilometres east of Hanoi.

It is located on the coast of the Gulf of Tonkin and serves as an important commercial and industrial hub for the area.

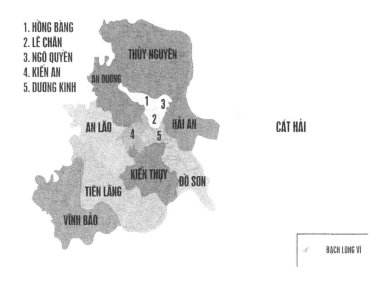

Other important cities in Vietnam include Da Nang, located in central Vietnam and it is the major port city; Can Tho is situated in the Mekong Delta region, it is the largest city in the delta and serves as the commercial and cultural hub of the area; and Nha Trang a coastal city in Khanh Hoa province, renowned for its stunning beaches and clear turquoise waters.

Da Nang City

INTRODUCTION

Vietnam is a nation situated in Southeast Asia, with a population of around 98 million people. It is surrounded by China to the north, Laos to the northwest, Cambodia to the southwest, and the South China Sea to the east.

The capital city is Hanoi, while the biggest city is Ho Chi Minh City (previously known as Saigon).

The nation has a rich and complicated history that extends back more than 4,000 years, with a strong cultural legacy that represents a blend of Chinese, French, and indigenous influences.

The Vietnamese language is the official language, however, many people also speak English, French, and Chinese.

In the 20th century, Vietnam went through a series of wars and conflicts, including the First Indochina War, the Vietnam War, and the Cambodian-Vietnamese War.

The Vietnam War, in particular, had a huge influence on the nation and its people, leading to social and economic turmoil, as well as environmental devastation.

Since the end of the Vietnam War in 1975, Vietnam has undergone significant economic and social changes, transitioning from a centrally-planned economy to a market-oriented economy.

Today, Vietnam is one of the fastest-growing economies in Southeast Asia, with a burgeoning middle class and a youthful and vibrant populace.

Tourism is a prominent sector in Vietnam, with sites such as Ha Long Bay, Hoi An Ancient Town, and the Cu Chi Tunnels bringing millions of tourists each year.

Vietnamese cuisine, famed for its use of fresh herbs, spices, and nuanced tastes, is also gaining favour across the globe.

In recent years, Vietnam has grown as a major actor in regional and global affairs, having strong relations with both the United States and China.

The country has also been actively engaged in several international organizations, including the United Nations, the Association of Southeast Asian Nations (ASEAN), and the World Trade Organization (WTO).

Despite the challenges that Vietnam has faced throughout its history, the country has shown remarkable resilience and has made significant progress in recent years.

As it continues to expand and develop, Vietnam is set to remain an important role in the region and on the world scene.

This "Travel Guide to Vietnam in 2023" is a useful tool for everyone wanting to visit Vietnam.

The book includes a complete introduction to the nation, its culture, history, and geography, as well as practical information on travel logistics, lodging, and activities.

The book is arranged into numerous parts that address different elements of travelling in Vietnam.

The first part gives an introduction to the nation and its inhabitants, providing readers with a general idea of what to anticipate.

This section also provides a thorough comment on why visiting Vietnam in 2023 is a fantastic idea.

The second part addresses trip logistics, including information on visas, transportation, and housing.

This section gives readers practical tips on how to plan their vacation, what to pack, and how to manage the country's transportation system.

The third half of the book is devoted to the country's key attractions, including Hanoi, Ho Chi Minh City, Halong Bay, Sapa, and the Mekong Delta.

Each place is explored in depth, including information on the best time to visit, top attractions, and local experiences.

The fourth half of the book includes cultural and historical places, including museums, temples, and landmarks. This part gives readers a greater grasp of Vietnam's diverse history and cultural heritage.

The fifth portion of the book concentrates on outdoor activities and adventure, including hiking, riding, and water sports.

Readers may discover thorough information on the best areas to participate in these activities, as well as practical tips on how to prepare for them.

Finally, the book contains a section on food and drink, covering the country's renowned meals, street food, and local delicacies.

Readers will get advice on where to eat, what to try, and how to navigate the country's culinary scene.

INTERESTING FACT ABOUT VIETNAM

1. **Name Origins**: The term "Vietnam" is a mixture of two words: "Viet" refers to the majority ethnic group in the country, and "Nam" means "south."

2. **Longevity**: Vietnam has one of the greatest life expectancies in Southeast Asia, with an average life expectancy of about 75 years.

3. **Tet Nguyen Dan**: The most significant and widely celebrated celebration in Vietnam is Tet Nguyen Dan, also known as the Vietnamese Lunar New Year. It is a time for family reunions, eating, and paying reverence to ancestors.

4. **Scooter Capital**: Vietnam boasts a high number of scooters and motorcycles per capita. It has been estimated that there are over 45 million registered motorcycles in the nation.

5. **National outfit**: The traditional outfit for ladies in Vietnam is called "Ao Dai," a long tunic worn over wide-legged slacks. It is considered a sign of elegance and grace.

6. **Reunification Express**: The Reunification Express is a railway line that travels from Hanoi in the north to Ho Chi Minh City in the south. It spans a distance of around 1,726 kilometres (1,072 miles) and provides spectacular views of Vietnam's countryside.

7. **Megacities**: Vietnam contains two megacities, which are cities with populations surpassing 10 million people: Hanoi in the north and Ho Chi Minh City in the south.

8. **Floating Markets**: The Mekong Delta in southern Vietnam is famed for its floating markets, where sellers sell things from boats. It's a dynamic and colourful atmosphere, delivering a unique shopping experience.

9. **National Animal**: The water buffalo is considered the national animal of Vietnam. It signifies hard labour, courage, and endurance in Vietnamese culture.

10. **Motorbike World Record**: Vietnam holds the Guinness World Record for the biggest person motorbike formation. In

2012, 2,368 motorcycle motorcyclists assembled in Ho Chi Minh City to make the shape.

11. **Coffee Egg:** One famous Vietnamese coffee variety is ca phe trung, often known as egg coffee. It is produced by mixing egg yolks with condensed milk and coffee, creating a creamy and sweet beverage.

12. **Conical Hats:** The famous conical hat, known as "non la," is a traditional hat worn by many Vietnamese people, particularly in rural regions. It gives protection from the sun and rain.

13. **Floating Islands:** The Mekong Delta is home to the rare phenomenon of floating islands called "cau khi." These are masses of plants that float on the river's surface and move with the currents.

14. **Incense hamlet:** The hamlet of Quang Phu Cau, near Hanoi, is recognized for its traditional trade of producing incense.

It generates a substantial amount of Vietnam's incense sticks, which are utilized in religious rites and rituals.

15. **National Symbols:** The national flower of Vietnam is the lotus, which signifies purity and beauty. The national animal, as indicated previously, is the water buffalo.

16. **Vietnamese Zodiac:** The Vietnamese zodiac is based on a 12-year cycle, with each year represented by an animal.

The animals include the rat, buffalo, tiger, cat, dragon, snake, horse, goat, monkey, rooster, dog, and pig.

17. **Fish Sauce:** Fish sauce, known as "nuoc mam," is a fundamental condiment in Vietnamese cuisine. It is prepared from fermented fish and lends a particular savoury taste to various foods.

18. **Fan-making hamlet:** The hamlet of Dong Ho is famed for its traditional handmade fans.

These fans are constructed from natural materials and include detailed folk art paintings showing scenes from everyday life and Vietnamese culture.

BRIEF HISTORY OF VIETNAM

Vietnam, formerly known as the Socialist Republic of Vietnam, is a Southeast Asian nation situated on the eastern Indochinese Peninsula.

Its history is rich and diverse, with a vast and diversified cultural legacy, as well as a stormy past defined by foreign invasions, battles, and attempts for freedom.

Here is a thorough review of Vietnam's history:

1. Ancient History

Prehistoric Period: Archaeological evidence supports human occupancy in

Vietnam as early as the Paleolithic Age, roughly 500,000 years ago.

Dong Son civilisation: From roughly 1000 BCE until the 3rd century CE, the Dong Son civilisation flourished in what is now northern Vietnam.

This time saw the development of superior bronze casting processes and the fabrication of elaborate bronze drums.

2. Chinese Domination

Early Chinese Influence: Vietnam fell under Chinese influence around the 2nd century BCE when the Han Dynasty invaded the area.

This marked the beginning of a thousand-year era of Chinese supremacy.

Trung Sisters' Rebellion: In the 1st century CE, the Trung sisters conducted a successful insurrection against Chinese control, temporarily creating an independent Vietnamese kingdom.

Phases of Resistance: Throughout the subsequent decades, Vietnam saw phases of resistance against Chinese authority, such as the rebellion led by Ly Bon in the 8th century and the uprising of Ngo Quyen in the 10th century.

3. Imperial Vietnam

Independence and Expansion: In 938 CE, Ngo Quyen overcame the Chinese soldiers, resulting in Vietnam's independence.

The ensuing centuries saw the growth of Vietnamese lands southward.

Tran and Le Dynasties: The Tran Dynasty (1225-1400) and the subsequent Le Dynasty (1428-1788) characterized a time of stability and cultural progress, with developments in literature, art, and governance.

Mongol Invasions: In the late 13th century, Vietnam successfully repulsed Mongol invasions by the Yuan Dynasty of China.

4. European Contact and Colonial Rule

The arrival of European Powers: European merchants, notably the Portuguese, Spanish, Dutch, and French, came to Vietnam from the 16th century onwards, establishing commercial stations.

French Colonialism: In the late 19th century, France steadily colonized Vietnam, Laos, and Cambodia, together constituting French Indochina.

The colonial process resulted in enormous social and economic changes and opposition groups.

5. Struggle for Independence

Rise of Nationalism: Vietnamese nationalism flourished during the early 20th century, with the development of groups like the Vietnamese Nationalist Party (VNQDĐ) and the Indochinese Communist Party (ICP).

World War II and the Viet Minh: During World War II, Japan seized Vietnam, and the Viet Minh, headed by Ho Chi Minh, emerged as the major rebel force against both Japanese invaders and French colonial power.

First Indochina War: After Japan's capitulation in 1945, Ho Chi Minh proclaimed Vietnamese independence, initiating the First Indochina War (1946-1954) between the Viet Minh and French troops.

The war concluded with the French loss at the Battle of Dien Bien Phu.

6. Vietnam War and Reunification

Division of Vietnam: The Geneva Accords of 1954 separated Vietnam along the 17th parallel, establishing the communist North and the anti-communist South.

Vietnam War: The Vietnam War (1955-1975) was a lengthy battle between North Vietnam (backed by the Soviet Union and China) and South Vietnam (supported by the United States and other anti-communist states).

The conflict resulted in great loss of life and substantial devastation.

7. Reunification and Post-War Vietnam

Fall of Saigon: In 1975, North Vietnamese troops, known as the People's Army of Vietnam (PAVN), conquered Saigon (now Ho Chi Minh City), resulting in the reunification of North and South Vietnam.

The war concluded with the triumph of the communist forces, and Vietnam became a united nation under the leadership of the Socialist Republic of Vietnam.

Post-War obstacles: After the war, Vietnam faced various obstacles, including the reunification of North and South, economic rehabilitation, and the effect of the conflict on society. The nation also suffered diplomatic isolation and a failing economy.

Doi Moi changes: In the late 1980s, Vietnam conducted economic changes known as Doi Moi, shifting from a centrally planned economy to a market-oriented socialist system.

These changes resulted in tremendous economic development and boosted international investment.

Normalization of ties: In the 1990s, Vietnam started on a road of diplomatic engagement and sought the normalization of ties with the international community, particularly the United States.

The relaxation of trade embargoes and the creation of diplomatic contacts helped Vietnam integrate into the global economy.

8. Modern Vietnam

Economic Development: Since the introduction of Doi Moi reforms, Vietnam has enjoyed tremendous economic growth and development.

It has emerged as one of the fastest-growing economies in Southeast Asia, with a concentration on manufacturing, services, and tourism.

Political Landscape: Vietnam remains a socialist republic with a single-party system run by the Communist Party of Vietnam (CPV).

However, there have been initiatives towards minimal political changes and improved openness to international business.

Regional Cooperation: Vietnam actively participates in regional organizations such as the Association of Southeast Asian

Nations (ASEAN) and has been involved in various regional initiatives, including the ASEAN Economic Community and the Comprehensive and Progressive Agreement for Trans-Pacific Partnership (CPTPP).

Socio-cultural Progress: Vietnam has made considerable gains in improving education, healthcare, and social welfare.

The country has also conserved and promoted its cultural legacy, including traditional arts, music, and food, which have received worldwide attention.

CHAPTER 1

TRIP PLANNING TO VIETNAM

This section includes key aspects such as when to go, admission procedures and visas, budgeting, health and safety concerns, and travel insurance.

Additionally, you will discover how to get to Vietnam and navigate the country's transportation system efficiently.

1.1 When To Travel To Vietnam

Choosing the perfect time to visit Vietnam will considerably improve your vacation experience. The climate of Vietnam is varied, with various locations experiencing unique weather patterns. Therefore, when planning your trip to Vietnam, it's important to consider the best time to visit each region.

In the northern part of Vietnam, the weather is often split into four seasons, including spring (March to May), summer (June to August), autumn (September to November), and winter (December to February).

The ideal season to visit this area is between spring (March to May) and fall (September to November), since the weather is moderate, dry, and comfortable.

During winter, it may be fairly chilly, with temperatures plummeting to 0°C, while summer can be hot and humid.

The central area of Vietnam, including towns like Hue and Hoi An, enjoys a tropical climate, with a rainy season from September to December and a dry season from January to August.

The greatest time to visit this area is from February through May when the weather is dry and warm.

In the southern part of Vietnam, which encompasses Ho Chi Minh City and the Mekong Delta, the weather is tropical, with two distinct seasons.

The rainy season is from May to November and the dry season is from December to April.

The greatest time to visit this area is from December to April when the weather is dry and agreeable.

Determining when to travel to Vietnam depends on the precise place you want to visit and the sort of weather you enjoy.

It's crucial to evaluate the weather trends of each place thoroughly and plan your vacation appropriately.

1.1.1 Map Showing When to Travel to Most Attractive Destinations in Vietnam

Below is a map of the most attractive destinations in Vietnam and the best time to visit them.

1.2 Journey To Vietnam

The two major international airports in Vietnam are Noi Bai in Hanoi and Tan Son Nhat in Ho Chi Minh City.

Many airlines offer flights to these airports, including Vietnam Airlines, Jetstar Pacific, and VietJet Air.
You may also enter Vietnam overland from Cambodia, Laos, or China.

1.2.1 Journeying to Vietnam from Cambodia

There are numerous routes you may take to go from Cambodia to Vietnam, depending on your starting place and your eventual destination in Vietnam.

The most common border crossings for overland travel are Bavet-Moc Bai and Ha Tien-Xa Xia.

Route 1: Phnom Penh to Ho Chi Minh City via Bavet-Moc Bai Border Crossing

This is the most direct route from Phnom Penh to Ho Chi Minh City.

You may take a bus or minivan from Phnom Penh to the border town of Bavet, which takes roughly 2-3 hours.

From there, you will need to walk over the border to the Vietnamese side and take another bus or minivan to Ho Chi Minh City, which takes another 2-3 hours.

The travel may take roughly 6-8 hours in total, depending on traffic and border crossing time.

Route 2: Siem Reap to Ho Chi Minh City via Bavet-Moc Bai Border Crossing

If you are beginning your travel from Siem Reap, you may take a bus or minivan from Siem Reap to Phnom Penh, which takes roughly 6-8 hours.

Once you arrive in Phnom Penh, you can continue your journey to Ho Chi Minh City via the Bavet-Moc Bai border crossing, as described in Route 1.

Route 3: Phnom Penh to Ho Chi Minh City via Chau Doc

This route takes you through the Mekong Delta area of Vietnam and is an excellent alternative for people who wish to visit the Delta region.

You may take a bus or minivan from Phnom Penh to the border town of Chau Doc, which takes roughly 5-6 hours. From there, you may take a speedboat to Ho Chi Minh City, which takes roughly 5-6 hours.

The travel may take roughly 10-12 hours in total, depending on traffic and border crossing time.

Route 4: Phnom Penh to Ha Tien via Prek Chak Border Crossing

This route takes you down the southern coast of Cambodia and is a wonderful choice for people who wish to explore the coastal area.

You may take a bus or minivan from Phnom Penh to the border town of Prek Chak, which takes roughly 4-5 hours.

From there, you will need to walk over the border to the Vietnamese side and take another bus or minivan to Ha Tien, which takes roughly 1-2 hours.

The travel may take roughly 6-7 hours in total, depending on traffic and border crossing time.

Route 5: Sihanoukville to Ha Tien via Prek Chak Border Crossing

If you are beginning your journey from Sihanoukville, you may take a bus or minivan from Sihanoukville to Kampot, which takes roughly 2-3 hours.

From there, you may take another bus or minivan to the border town of Prek Chak, as indicated in Route 4.

Once you cross the border, you can continue your journey to Ha Tien, as described in Route 4.

It's crucial to know that the road conditions in Cambodia and Vietnam may be tough, and the border crossings can be time-consuming.

It's better to plan your route and to give plenty of time for unanticipated delays. It's also crucial to have all the relevant travel paperwork, including your passport, visa, and any needed immunizations.

1.2.2 Journeying to Vietnam from Laos

Here is a guide on how to travel to Vietnam by road from Laos

Route 1: From Vientiane to Hanoi

From Vientiane, take a bus or private automobile to Vinh (in Nghe An province, Vietnam), which is roughly a 10-hour journey.
From Vinh, take a bus or train to Hanoi, which is around a 3-5 hour trip.

Route 2: From Luang Prabang to Hanoi

From Luang Prabang, take a bus or private automobile to Dien Bien Phu (in Vietnam), which is around a 10-12 hour ride.

From Dien Bien Phu, take a bus or private automobile to Hanoi, which is around an 8-10 hour ride.

Route 3: From Pakse to Ho Chi Minh City

From Pakse, take a bus or private vehicle to Savannakhet (in Laos), which is roughly a 4-6 hour ride.

From Savannakhet, take a bus or private vehicle to Lao Bao (in Vietnam), which is around a 5-6 hour ride.

From Lao Bao, take a bus or private vehicle to Hue or Da Nang, then to Ho Chi Minh City via rail or bus.

Route 4: From Savannakhet to Hue

From Savannakhet, take a bus or private vehicle to Lao Bao (in Vietnam), which is around a 5-6 hour ride.

From Lao Bao, take a bus or private vehicle to Hue, which is around a 3-4 hour ride.

Route 5: From Vientiane to Hue or Da Nang

From Vientiane, take a bus or private automobile to Vinh (in Nghe An province,

Vietnam), which is roughly a 10-hour journey.

From Vinh, take a bus or train to Hue or Da Nang.

1.2.3 Getting to Vietnam from China

Route 1: From Nanning to Hanoi

From Nanning, take a bus or private automobile to the Friendship Pass border post (at the border between China and Vietnam).

Cross the border and enter Vietnam.
Take a bus or private automobile to Hanoi, which is around a 4-5 hour trip.

Route 2: From Kunming to Hanoi

From Kunming, take a train or bus to the border town of Hekou.

Cross the border and enter Vietnam.

Take a bus or private automobile to Hanoi, which is around a 14-15 hour trip.

Route 3: From Mengzi to Lao Cai

From Mengzi, take a train or bus to the border town of Hekou.

Cross the border and enter Vietnam.

Take a bus or private vehicle to Lao Cai, which is around a 1-2 hour ride.

Route 4: From Pingxiang to Hanoi

From Pingxiang, take a bus or private automobile to the Dong Dang border post (near the border between China and Vietnam).

Cross the border and enter Vietnam.

Take a bus or private automobile to Hanoi, which is around a 3-4 hour trip.

Route 5: From Honghe to Lao Cai

From Honghe, take a bus or private automobile to the Hekou border post (near the border between China and Vietnam).

Cross the border and enter Vietnam.

Take a bus or private vehicle to Lao Cai, which is around a 1-2 hour ride.

Route 6: From Zhanjiang to Haiphong

From Zhanjiang, take a boat to Haiphong, Vietnam.

This route is less usual, but it gives an alternate method to go to Vietnam from China by water.

Note that certain routes may have various border-crossing processes and regulations, so it is crucial to verify with the appropriate authorities and to have all required documentation in order before beginning these excursions.

Additionally, the road conditions in some areas may be rough, so it is important to plan for longer travel times and to bring the necessary supplies for the journey.

1.3 Entry Requirements and Visa

To enter Vietnam, most foreign people need a valid passport and a visa. However, there are some exceptions to this requirement for citizens of certain countries who are eligible for visa-free entry or visa-on-arrival.

Here are some key details to keep in mind regarding entry requirements and visas for Vietnam

1.3.1 Passport

All foreign nationals must have a valid passport that is valid for at least six months after the date of admission into Vietnam.

1.3.2 Visa

Most foreign nationals need a visa to enter Vietnam. There are numerous sorts of visas available, including tourist visas, business visas, and student visas.

Tourist visas are permitted for stays of up to 30 days, whereas business visas might be valid for up to 90 days or longer.

1.3.3 Visa exemptions

Citizens of certain countries are exempt from the visa requirement for stays of a specific period.

For example, citizens of ASEAN nations, South Korea, Japan, and several European countries may visit Vietnam without a visa for durations of up to 15-90 days, depending on their nationality.

1.3.4 Visa-on-arrival

For individuals who need a visa to visit Vietnam, a visa-on-arrival option is available for those going by plane.

This enables tourists to apply for a visa online and get a pre-approval letter that may be used to secure a visa upon arrival at the airport in Vietnam.

1.3.5 Visa extension

For individuals who intend to remain in Vietnam for a longer term, it is feasible to extend a visa in-country. This procedure involves an application and associated expenses.

It's crucial to remember that entrance criteria and visa laws might vary, so it's encouraged to verify the latest information from the Vietnamese embassy or consulate in your home country before visiting.

Additionally, it's important to ensure that you have all the necessary documents and visas before travelling to Vietnam to avoid any issues with immigration.

1.4 Currency and Budgeting

Vietnam's official currency is the Vietnamese dong (VND). However, US dollars are widely accepted in tourist areas, and some hotels and restaurants may also accept payment in euros or other major currencies.

It is advisable to carry some cash in VND for everyday costs and to convert money at banks or authorized exchange businesses to receive a better exchange rate.

When budgeting for a trip to Vietnam, it's important to consider the cost of transportation, accommodation, food, activities, and souvenirs.

Here are some rough estimates of the costs you can expect in Vietnam

Accommodation

Budget hotels and guesthouses may be obtained for as low as $10-20 per night.

Mid-range hotels and resorts vary from $30-100 per night, while luxury hotels may cost $200 or more per night.

Food

Street food and small eateries provide some of the most economical alternatives for meals in Vietnam, with dishes costing as low as $1-2. Mid-range and premium restaurants might cost $10-20 or more for each meal.

Transportation

Public transportation in Vietnam is reasonably economical, with buses, trains, and taxis accessible in most cities.

A cab journey in Hanoi or Ho Chi Minh City normally costs between $5-10.

Motorbike rentals are very popular and may cost roughly $5-10 per day.

Activities

Entrance fees for famous tourist destinations like Halong Bay, the Cu Chi Tunnels, and the Mekong Delta may vary from $5-20. Day trips and excursions might cost anywhere from $20-100 or more, depending on the activity.

1.5 Health and Safety Considerations

Here are the health and safety considerations

Vaccines

Make sure you are up-to-date on normal vaccines, such as measles, mumps, and rubella (MMR), and consider being immunized against illnesses that are more frequent in Vietnam, including hepatitis A and B, typhoid, and Japanese encephalitis.

Food and Water

Be vigilant about what you eat and drink, since contaminated food and water may cause diseases such as traveller's diarrhoea. Stick to bottled water and avoid ice cubes or raw or undercooked meals.

Mosquitoes and Other Insects

Protect yourself from mosquito-borne diseases such as dengue fever and malaria by wearing insect repellent and long-sleeved clothes. If you are going to rural regions, consider taking anti-malaria medicine.

Traffic and Road Safety

Traffic in Vietnam may be chaotic, with many drivers breaking traffic rules and regulations. Be extra cautious while crossing roadways and consider wearing a helmet if you want to hire a motorcycle.

Scams and Petty Crimes

Petty crimes such as pickpocketing and stealing may be a concern in busy locations such as markets and tourist destinations.

Be careful and keep an eye on your valuables. Also, be wary of scams such as fake taxi drivers or inflated prices for goods and services.

Natural catastrophes

Vietnam is prone to natural catastrophes such as typhoons, floods, and landslides, particularly during the rainy season from May to November.

Stay informed about weather conditions and follow the advice of local authorities.

1.6 Travel Insurance

Vietnam travel insurance is a sort of travel insurance that exclusively protects tourists who are going to visit Vietnam.

It offers coverage for a variety of travel-related difficulties, such as medical bills, trip cancellations or delays, lost or stolen baggage, and emergency evacuations.

Here are some crucial things to know about Vietnam travel insurance

Coverage

Vietnam travel insurance often includes coverage for medical bills, emergency medical transportation, trip cancellations or interruptions, lost or stolen baggage, and personal liability.

Some policies may also include coverage for travel delays, rental car damage, and other issues.

Medical Expenses

Vietnam travel insurance may assist cover the expense of medical care if you get ill or injured while travelling in Vietnam. This can include hospitalization, emergency medical transportation, and other related expenses.

Vacation Cancellations or Interruptions

If you need to cancel or cut short your vacation due to unforeseen occurrences such as sickness, accident, or natural catastrophes, Vietnam travel insurance may assist to cover the expenses of non-refundable travel arrangements.

Lost or Stolen baggage

If your baggage is lost, stolen, or damaged during your vacation to Vietnam, travel insurance may give payment for the cost of the lost or damaged goods.

Emergency Evacuations

If you need to be evacuated from Vietnam due to a medical emergency or other unexpected circumstances, Vietnam travel insurance may cover the cost of emergency transportation and medical care.

Natural catastrophes

Vietnam is prone to natural catastrophes such as typhoons, floods, and landslides. Some travel insurance policies may include coverage for these types of events.

Company Reputation

When picking a Vietnam travel insurance policy, it's crucial to find a reputed company with a track record of offering great coverage and customer care.

Exclusions and restrictions

It's crucial to study the policy carefully and be aware of any exclusions or restrictions on coverage, such as pre-existing medical problems or specific activities that are not covered.

Cost

Consider the cost of the insurance and if it delivers excellent value for the coverage given.

Some policies may be more expensive but offer more comprehensive coverage, while others may be cheaper but have more exclusions and limitations.

CHAPTER 2

THE REGIONS AND CITIES IN VIETNAM

Vietnam is split into eight areas, each having its own distinct culture, geography, and history.

The regions include the Red River Delta, Northeast, Northwest, North Central Coast, South Central Coast, Central Highlands, Southeast, and Mekong River Delta.

Vietnam includes numerous important cities, including the capital city of Hanoi, the economic centre of Ho Chi Minh City (commonly known as Saigon), the seaside city of Da Nang, and the historic city of Hue.

Other prominent cities include Nha Trang, Phan Thiet, and the Mekong Delta centre of Can Tho.

Each city has its charms and character, making Vietnam a unique and intriguing nation to visit.

2.1 Red River Delta Region

The Red River Delta area is situated in the northern section of Vietnam and is called the Red River, which passes through the area. It is one of the most populated and developed areas in the nation, with a rich history and lively culture.

The area comprises eleven provinces and municipalities, including the capital city of Hanoi, as well as Haiphong, Hai Duong,

Hung Yen, Nam Dinh, Ninh Binh, Thai Binh, Bac Giang, Bac Ninh, Hoa Binh, and Vinh Phuc.

The Red River Delta is recognized for its lush agricultural soil, which supports a range of crops including rice, vegetables, fruits, and fish. The area also has a rich history of handicrafts, including traditional pottery, silk weaving, and wood carving.

2.2 Northeast Region

The Northeast Region is situated in the northern region of Vietnam, bordering China to the north and east. It is a hilly location with steep terrain and is noted for its natural beauty and rich cultural legacy.

The area contains nine provinces, namely Bac Kan, Bac Giang, Cao Bang, Ha

Giang, Lang Son, Phu Tho, Quang Ninh, Thai Nguyen, and Tuyen Quang.

The Northeast Region is home to various ethnic minority groups, including the Tay, Nung, Dao, and Hmong, each with its own unique culture and customs.

The area is also noted for its historic attractions, including the UNESCO World Heritage Site of Ha Long Bay, as well as old temples and pagodas.

The region's economy is predominantly agricultural, with rice, tea, and rubber being the principal crops. Mining is also a key business, with coal and other minerals being produced in various provinces.

2.3 Northwest Region

The Northwest Region is situated in the rugged northern portion of Vietnam, bordering China to the north and west. The area is noted for its mountainous topography, scenic scenery, and different ethnic cultures.

The Northwest Region comprises five provinces, including Hoa Binh, Son La, Dien Bien, Lai Chau, and Yen Bai.

The area is home to various ethnic minority groups, including the Hmong, Dao, Thai, and Muong, each having its unique language, customs, and traditions.

The region's economy is mostly centred on agriculture, with rice, maize, and other crops being farmed in the valleys and lower altitudes, and cattle being kept in the higher elevations. The area is also rich in natural resources, including lumber, coal, and minerals.

The Northwest Region is a renowned tourist destination, recognized for its gorgeous scenery, including terraced rice fields, verdant woods, and mountain peaks.

The area is also home to several cultural and historical monuments, notably the Dien Bien Phu battlefield, where the Vietnamese defeated the French in 1954.

2.4 North Central Coast Region

The North Central Coast Region of Vietnam is a short strip of land that spans along the country's central coast.

It is located between the Northeast Region and the South Central Coast Region and is noted for its gorgeous beaches, historic attractions, and various cultures.

The North Central Coast Region encompasses six provinces, namely Thanh Hoa, Nghe An, Ha Tinh, Quang Binh, Quang Tri, and Thua Thien Hue.

The region's scenery boasts a blend of mountains, rivers, and beaches, making it a popular location for outdoor activities like hiking, camping, and water sports.

The area is also rich in history, with numerous cultural and historical landmarks, notably the old capital of Hue, which is home to the UNESCO World Heritage Site of the Imperial Citadel and Royal Tombs.

Other notable destinations include the Phong Nha-Ke Bang National Park in Quang Binh province, famed for its magnificent caverns and karst formations.

The North Central Coast Region's economy is built mostly on agriculture, with rice being the predominant crop. Fishing is also a major business, with many coastal towns dependent on it for their lives.

In recent years, the area has also witnessed substantial expansion in tourism, with numerous new hotels, resorts, and attractions being erected.

Visitors to the North Central Coast Region may enjoy a combination of outdoor activities, cultural experiences, and leisure on some of Vietnam's most stunning beaches.

2.5 South Central Coast Region

The South Central Coast Region of Vietnam is a small strip of territory that extends along the country's central coast, ranging from Binh Thuan Province in the south to Phu Yen Province in the north.

The area is noted for its spectacular beaches, attractive scenery, and rich cultural history.

The South Central Coast Region encompasses seven provinces, namely Binh Dinh, Da Nang, Khanh Hoa, Ninh Thuan, Phu Yen, Quang Nam, and Quang Ngai.

The area is home to several major historical and cultural landmarks, notably the Cham towers of My Son in Quang Nam province, and the old town of Hoi An, a UNESCO World Heritage Site.

The region's economy is built mostly on agriculture, with rice, coffee, and cashew nuts being the primary crops. Fishing is also a major business, with many coastal towns dependent on it for their lives.

In recent years, tourism has been a key contributor to the region's economy, with people flocking to enjoy the region's gorgeous beaches, water sports, and cultural attractions.

The South Central Coast Region is home to some of Vietnam's most stunning beaches, including Nha Trang Beach in

Khanh Hoa province and Mui Ne Beach in Binh Thuan province.

The area is also recognized for its rough mountains and national parks, such as the Kon Tum and Nui Chua national parks.

2.6 Central Highlands Region

The Central Highlands area of Vietnam is a hilly area situated in the southern half of the nation. It is recognized for its lush woods, stunning waterfalls, and different ethnic cultures.

The Central Highlands Region encompasses five provinces, namely Dak Lak, Dak Nong, Gia Lai, Kon Tum, and Lam Dong.

The area is home to various ethnic minority groups, including the Bahnar, Ede, and Jarai, each with its distinct language, customs, and traditions.

The region's economy is built mostly on agriculture, with coffee, rubber, and pepper being the primary crops. The area is also rich in natural resources, including minerals, wood, and animals.

The Central Highlands Region is a famous tourist destination, recognized for its natural beauty and cultural variety.

Visitors may visit the region's national parks, such as Yok Don and Cat Tien, which are home to numerous rare and endangered species.

The area is particularly notable for its waterfalls, such as the Dray Nur and Dray Sap waterfalls in Dak Lak province.

The city of Da Lat in Lam Dong province is a popular tourist attraction, noted for its mild environment, French colonial architecture, and stunning surroundings.

Other popular attractions in the region include the Buon Ma Thuot coffee museum in Dak Lak province and the Kon Tum wooden church in Kon Tum province.

2.7 Southeast Region

The Southeast Region of Vietnam is a lively and diversified region situated in the southern section of the nation. It is recognized for its vibrant cities, magnificent beaches, and rich history.

The Southeast Region encompasses six provinces, namely Ba Ria-Vung Tau, Binh Duong, Binh Phuoc, Dong Nai, Tay Ninh, and Ho Chi Minh City. The region's economy is one of the most developed in Vietnam, with a concentration on industry, services, and tourism.

2.8 Mekong River Delta Region

The Mekong River Delta Region of Vietnam is a huge and rich region situated in the southern section of the nation. It is recognized for its lush agricultural area, bustling floating markets, and extensive canals.

The Mekong River Delta Region encompasses 13 provinces, including Can Tho, Vinh Long, Soc Trang, and An Giang. The area is home to nearly 17 million people, making it one of the most densely inhabited regions in Vietnam.

The region's economy is focused mostly on agriculture, with rice, fruit, and shellfish being the primary products. The area is also noted for its handicrafts, including weaving and ceramics.

The Mekong River Delta Region is famed for its floating marketplaces, where sellers sell their items from boats along the river.

Visitors may also visit the region's picturesque waterways, such as the Cai Rang and Phong Dien canals in May Tho City.

The area is also home to various cultural and historical landmarks, including the Sam Mountain in An Giang province and the Khmer pagodas in Soc Trang province.

CHAPTER 3

TOP CITIES ACCOMMODATION OPTIONS FOR TOURISTS IN VIETNAM

Vietnam provides a broad selection of hotel alternatives for guests to meet all budgets and interests.

Here are some of the most common types of accommodation available in Vietnam

3.1 Top Hotels for Tourists in Hanoi City

3.1.1 The Sofitel Legend Metropole Hanoi

The Sofitel Legend Metropole Hanoi is a prominent and historic five-star hotel situated in the centre of Hanoi, Vietnam.

With its historic past, great service, and lavish facilities, the hotel is considered as one of the best hotels in the city.

Here are some significant characteristics and aspects of the Sofitel Legend Metropole Hanoi:

1. Historical Significance: The hotel goes back to 1901 and has played a key part in Hanoi's history. It has received countless international leaders, celebrities, and prominent persons over the years, contributing to its appeal and significance.

2. Colonial Architecture and Elegance: The hotel merges historic French colonial architecture with Vietnamese characteristics, creating a distinctive and appealing ambience. The immaculately restored façade and interior reflect the hotel's long legacy and timeless beauty.

3. Accommodation: The Sofitel Legend Metropole Hanoi provides a selection of elegant rooms and suites that flawlessly integrate traditional charm with contemporary amenities.

Each room is elegantly appointed and has high-end furniture, soft bedding, and state-of-the-art conveniences, assuring a pleasant and memorable stay.

4. Outstanding Dining Experiences: The hotel is recognized for its outstanding dining offerings. Guests may indulge in excellent French cuisine at Le Beaulieu, discover traditional Vietnamese specialities at Spices Garden, or enjoy a relaxing afternoon tea at Le Club.

The hotel's restaurants and bars deliver outstanding gastronomic experiences in attractive surroundings.

5. Le Spa du Metropole: The hotel's spa is a refuge of tranquillity and renewal. Inspired by ancient Vietnamese traditions and current health practices, the spa provides a variety of treatments, massages, and therapies.

Guests may rest and unwind in the calm atmosphere while experienced therapists give individualized treatment.

6. Legendary Service: Sofitel Legend Metropole Hanoi is recognized for its exceptional service and attention to detail. The committed team goes above and beyond to ensure that every guest's requirements are satisfied, offering customized service and creating a memorable and luxurious experience.

7. Central Location: Situated in the historic French Quarter, the hotel gives easy access to Hanoi's key attractions, including Hoan Kiem Lake, the Old Quarter, and the Hanoi Opera House.

Guests may easily explore the city's cultural monuments and bustling streets from this great location.

3.1.2 The Oriental Jade Hotel

The Oriental Jade Hotel is a magnificent boutique hotel situated in the heart of Hanoi's Old Quarter, Vietnam. With its contemporary architecture, customized service, and great location, it gives visitors a fashionable and comfortable base to explore the city.

Here are some main characteristics and attractions of The Oriental Jade Hotel:

1. Stylish and Contemporary Design: The hotel offers a sleek and modern design, integrating Vietnamese aesthetics with contemporary elements.

The interior has stylish furniture, creative details, and a coordinated colour palette, providing a visually attractive and pleasant ambience.

2. Accommodation: The Oriental Jade Hotel provides a choice of well-appointed rooms and suites constructed with comfort and elegance in mind.

Each room is beautifully furnished and outfitted with contemporary conveniences, including luxurious beds, flat-screen TVs, and free Wi-Fi. Some rooms additionally provide city views or private balconies.

3. Rooftop Sky Bar and Restaurant: The hotel's rooftop Sky Bar and Restaurant offers a spectacular environment to enjoy panoramic views of Hanoi's cityscape while indulging in excellent drinks and a broad menu of Vietnamese and foreign cuisines.

It is a terrific spot to rest and unwind while taking in the city's dynamic vitality.

4. Wellness amenities: The Oriental Jade Hotel provides wellness amenities, including a fitness centre and a spa.

Guests may keep active and rejuvenate throughout their stay by working out at the gym or enjoying a choice of spa treatments, massages, and therapies supplied by experienced therapists.

5. Individual Service: The hotel prides itself on its service, ensuring that visitors feel welcome and well taken care of during their stay.

The attentive and pleasant personnel are committed to offering help, whether it's booking sightseeing trips, making restaurant suggestions, or fulfilling specific requests.

6. Central Location: The Oriental Jade Hotel is well placed in Hanoi's Old Quarter, famed for its lively streets, historic monuments, and dynamic ambience.

Guests may easily explore major landmarks like Hoan Kiem Lake, the Hanoi Opera House, and the Night Market, as well as enjoy the local stores, street cuisine, and cultural activities in the surrounding region.

3.1.3 Apricot Hotel

The Apricot Hotel is a luxurious boutique hotel situated in the centre of Hanoi, Vietnam. With its beautiful architecture, innovative idea, and great location, the hotel delivers a classy and unforgettable experience for discriminating tourists.

Here are some main characteristics and attractions of the Apricot Hotel:

1. Artistic Concept: The Apricot Hotel embraces the beauty of art and culture, with its design influenced by the masterpieces of Vietnamese painters.

The hotel presents a wide collection of unique artworks and sculptures throughout its public areas and guest rooms, providing a visually fascinating and culturally absorbing setting.

2. Accommodation: The hotel provides well-appointed rooms and suites that mix elegance with contemporary comfort.

Each room is built with care to detail and boasts elegant furniture, excellent amenities, and stunning views of the city or the hotel's courtyard. The rooms offer a calm escape for travellers after a day of touring Hanoi.

3. Art Gastronomy: The Apricot Hotel provides a unique gastronomic experience with its Art Gastronomy concept.

The hotel's restaurants, L'Artiste and Palette, feature a blend of foreign and Vietnamese cuisines, ingeniously presented as culinary artworks.

Guests may experience excellent cuisine while immersing themselves in the creative ambience.

4. Rooftop Pool and Bar: The hotel offers a rooftop infinity pool and bar, affording panoramic views of Hanoi's skyline. Guests may relax by the poolside, take a refreshing dip, or enjoy beverages and light nibbles while viewing the gorgeous cityscape.

5. Wellness and Fitness: The Apricot Hotel offers wellness and fitness facilities to boost visitors' well-being. The fitness facility is equipped with current equipment, enabling visitors to keep their workout program.

The spa provides a variety of treatments and therapies to encourage relaxation and regeneration.

6. Central Location: Situated in the heart of Hanoi's historic capital, the Apricot Hotel gives easy access to major sights such as Hoan Kiem Lake, the Old Quarter, and the Hanoi Opera House.

Guests may easily tour the city's cultural sites, lively streets, and colourful marketplaces.

7. Individual Service: The hotel is noted for its warm hospitality and individual service. The attentive staff ensures that every guest's requirements are satisfied, giving help with bookings, sightseeing suggestions, and any other requests to make the stay pleasurable and memorable.

3.1.4 La Siesta Diamond Hotel & Spa

La Siesta Diamond Hotel & Spa is a boutique hotel situated in the heart of Hanoi's Old Quarter, Vietnam.

With its lovely architecture, kind hospitality, and variety of services, the hotel provides a pleasant stay for guests.

Here are some important characteristics and attractions of La Siesta Diamond Hotel & Spa:

1. Beautiful and Elegant Design: The hotel offers a beautiful and elegant design, merging traditional Vietnamese features with modern accents.

The interior offers a blend of warm hues, wooden accents, and creative artwork, providing a pleasant and welcoming feel.

2. Accommodation: La Siesta Diamond Hotel & Spa provides well-appointed rooms and suites intended to give comfort and relaxation.

The rooms are elegantly furnished and equipped with contemporary conveniences, including comfortable linen, flat-screen TVs, and free Wi-Fi. Some rooms additionally include balconies with city views.

3. Dining Options: The hotel has a restaurant and a rooftop bar where guests can enjoy wonderful Vietnamese and foreign cuisine.

The restaurant provides a choice of meals cooked with fresh and locally produced ingredients, delivering a great gastronomic experience.

4. Spa & Wellness: The hotel's spa provides a selection of treatments and therapies aimed to refresh and soothe visitors.

From soothing massages to revitalizing facials, professional therapists give individualized treatment in a serene atmosphere, providing a joyful encounter.

5. Individual Service: La Siesta Diamond Hotel & Spa prides itself on its attentive and individual service.

The attentive staff goes the additional mile to ensure visitors' requirements are satisfied, from arranging airport transfers to aiding with tourist suggestions and planning excursions, making the stay hassle-free and pleasurable.

6. Central Location: Situated in Hanoi's dynamic Old Quarter, the hotel gives convenient access to major sights, marketplaces, and cultural sites.

Guests may explore the lively streets, see historical monuments, and enjoy the local culture and food with excellent ease.

7. Complimentary Services: La Siesta Diamond Hotel & Spa provides a selection of complimentary services, including daily breakfast, afternoon tea, and a welcome drink upon arrival.

These considerate enhancements improve the entire visitor experience and give additional value.

3.1.5 Hotel de l'Opera Hanoi - MGallery

Hotel de l'Opera Hanoi - MGallery is a magnificent five-star hotel situated in the historic French Quarter of Hanoi, Vietnam.

With its beautiful design, creative flair, and outstanding service, the hotel provides a refined and unforgettable stay for discriminating tourists.

Here are some important characteristics and attractions of Hotel de l'Opera Hanoi - MGallery:

1. French-inspired Design: The hotel emanates a French-inspired ambience with its exquisite architecture, classic interior design, and creative components.

The décor represents a combination of neoclassical and modern styles, providing a refined and aesthetically attractive ambience.

2. Accommodation: Hotel de l'Opera Hanoi provides large and well-appointed rooms and suites that blend comfort with contemporary facilities.

Each room is attractively designed and outfitted with comfortable bedding, high-quality linens, and state-of-the-art technology. Some rooms additionally provide views of the city or the hotel's courtyard.

3. Dining Experiences: The hotel features a range of dining choices that highlight culinary brilliance. Satine Restaurant provides a choice of Vietnamese and foreign meals created using locally sourced ingredients.

The La Fee Verte Bar delivers creative cocktails and quality wines in a sophisticated environment, while Café Lautrec offers a lovely assortment of pastries and drinks.

4. Le Spa du Metropole: The hotel's spa offers a tranquil and enjoyable escape for guests.

Le Spa du Metropole provides a variety of revitalizing treatments and therapies influenced by Vietnamese traditions and current health methods. Guests may rest, unwind, and revitalize in the quiet ambience of the spa.

5. The Club Lounge: Hotel de l'Opera Hanoi has an exclusive Club Lounge where guests may enjoy customized services and extra privileges.

The lounge provides free breakfast, afternoon tea, and evening drinks, along with a quiet place for leisure and socialization.

6. Cultural Experiences: The hotel arranges cultural experiences and events for visitors to learn about the local culture and history.

From guided tours to culinary workshops and cultural performances, visitors may immerse themselves in the rich traditions of Hanoi and Vietnam.

7. Prime Location: Situated in the centre of Hanoi's French Quarter, Hotel de l'Opera Hanoi provides easy access to major sights such as Hoan Kiem Lake, the Hanoi Opera House, and the Old Quarter.

Guests may easily tour the city's cultural sites, museums, galleries, and busy marketplaces.

3.2 Top Hotels for Tourists in Ho Chi Minh City (Saigon)

3.2.1 The Reverie Saigon

The Reverie Saigon is a magnificent five-star hotel situated in the centre of Ho Chi Minh City (Saigon), Vietnam. Known for its luxury, elegant design, and world-class services, the hotel delivers a rich and unforgettable experience for discriminating tourists.

Here are some main elements and attractions of The Reverie Saigon:

1. Unparalleled Luxury and Design: The Reverie Saigon is recognized for its unrivalled luxury and lavish design. The hotel has exquisite décor built by famous Italian designers, resulting in a stylish and aesthetically captivating ambience.

From the stately entrance to the guest suites, every detail oozes richness and refinement.

2. Sumptuous Accommodations: The hotel provides a selection of sumptuous and large rooms and suites that are precisely constructed and outfitted with the best furniture and services. Each room features distinctive décor, sophisticated furniture, and panoramic views of the city, offering a delightful and comfortable stay.

3. Gourmet eating Experiences: The Reverie Saigon is a gastronomic heaven with a range of great eating establishments.

Guests may enjoy a range of cuisines, including Italian food at R&J Italian Lounge & Restaurant, Cantonese delicacies at The Royal Pavilion, and European-inspired meals at Café Cardinal.

The hotel's dining selections provide an excellent gastronomic excursion for every palette.

4. Exclusive Spa & Wellness: The Reverie Spa is a refuge of relaxation and regeneration. Offering a complete variety of treatments and therapies, clients may pamper themselves with exquisite spa experiences suited to their tastes.

The state-of-the-art fitness facility and rooftop pool give extra possibilities for visitors to be active and relax.

5. Impeccable Service: The Reverie Saigon prides itself on offering superior and customized service to its customers.

The committed staff is attentive, and competent, and goes above and beyond to guarantee a memorable and effortless visit. From concierge services to in-room dining, every part of the guest experience is attended to the greatest attention.

6. Central position: Situated in the heart of District 1, The Reverie Saigon boasts a superb position in Ho Chi Minh City.

It gives quick access to important sites such as the Saigon Opera House, Notre Dame Cathedral, and the historic Dong Khoi Street. Guests may easily tour the colourful city and its cultural treasures.

7. Luxury Shopping at Times Square: The hotel is part of the historic Times Square Building, which is home to high-end luxury goods.

Guests may engage in a world-class shopping experience without leaving the grounds, with a selection of recognized fashion and jewellery brands accessible only steps away.

3.2.2 Park Hyatt Saigon

Park Hyatt Saigon is a prominent five-star hotel situated in the centre of Ho Chi Minh City (Saigon), Vietnam.

With its exquisite design, superb service, and sumptuous facilities, the hotel delivers a refined and upmarket experience for discriminating tourists.

Here are some main characteristics and attractions of Park Hyatt Saigon:

1. Exquisite and Contemporary Architectural: The hotel mixes exquisite colonial-style architecture with contemporary architectural features, creating a refined and timeless ambience.

The interior areas are carefully designed with a perfect combination of traditional Vietnamese accents and contemporary furniture.

2. Luxurious Accommodations: Park Hyatt Saigon provides large and contemporary rooms and suites intended to give optimum comfort and relaxation.

Each room is beautifully outfitted with sumptuous bedding, premium amenities, and contemporary technology, assuring a delightful and pleasurable stay for visitors.

3. Gastronomic Delights: The hotel has a range of culinary choices that appeal to every appetite. Opera Restaurant provides a varied variety of foreign foods, while Square One emphasizes Vietnamese and Western cuisine.

The hotel's bar, 2 Lam Son, is a classy venue to savour creative cocktails and excellent wines.

4. Xuan Spa: Park Hyatt Saigon boasts a magnificent spa that provides a variety of holistic treatments and therapies inspired by Vietnamese traditions.

Guests may enjoy restorative massages, facials, and body treatments in a calm and tranquil location, giving a pleasant retreat from the hectic metropolis.

5. Rooftop Pool & Fitness Center: The hotel's rooftop pool offers a calm haven for guests to relax and enjoy panoramic views of the city. The neighbouring fitness facility is outfitted with state-of-the-art equipment, enabling visitors to keep their exercise program throughout their stay.

6. Central Location: Situated in the centre of District 1, Park Hyatt Saigon gives easy access to major sights including the Opera House, Notre Dame Cathedral, and the historic Dong Khoi Street.

Guests may tour the colourful city and immerse themselves in its cultural monuments and busy marketplaces.

7. Personalized Service: The hotel prides itself on its superior service and attention to detail.

The devoted team is committed to offering customized service, ensuring that every guest's requirements are satisfied and their stay is memorable and pleasurable.

8. Meetings & Events amenities: Park Hyatt Saigon provides flexible event rooms and state-of-the-art amenities for holding meetings, conferences, weddings, and other special events.

The hotel's specialized events staff is ready to help in designing and executing outstanding events with accuracy and flair.

3.2.3 Caravelle Saigon

Caravelle Saigon is a prominent five-star hotel situated in the centre of Ho Chi Minh City (Saigon), Vietnam.

With its historic history, modern elegance, and great service, the hotel provides a luxury and unforgettable experience for discriminating tourists.

Here are some significant characteristics and attractions of Caravelle Saigon:

1. Historic Landmark: Caravelle Saigon maintains a distinct position in the city's history as one of its most famous monuments.

The hotel has been a witness to historic events and played home to various dignitaries, making it a symbol of Ho Chi Minh City's past.

2. Elegant Accommodations: The hotel provides well-appointed rooms and suites that integrate modern style with comfort and practicality.

Each room is large and professionally furnished, providing contemporary facilities, plush linen, and breathtaking views of the city or the Saigon River.

3. Gastronomic Excellence: Caravelle Saigon has a selection of dining options that appeal to varied palates.

Guests may indulge in world cuisine at Nineteen Restaurant, appreciate contemporary Vietnamese cuisine at Reflections Restaurant, or enjoy a rooftop dining experience at Saigon Saigon Rooftop Bar.

4. Famous Cocktail Bar: The hotel's famous Martini Bar is a favourite location for cocktail connoisseurs. With a comprehensive selection of beautifully made cocktails, customers may enjoy the colourful ambience and live entertainment while sipping on their favourite beverages.

5. Rooftop Pool and Fitness Center: The hotel offers a rooftop swimming pool, giving a tranquil retreat with panoramic views of the metropolitan skyline.

The nearby fitness facility is equipped with the latest equipment, enabling visitors to keep their exercise program throughout their stay.

6. Spa & Wellness: Caravelle Saigon's Kara Spa provides a selection of calming treatments and therapies to refresh the body and mind.

Guests may pamper themselves with sumptuous massages, facials, and body treatments, all performed by professional therapists in a calm and tranquil atmosphere.

7. Central Location: Situated in the centre of District 1, Caravelle Saigon gives convenient access to major sights including the Opera House, Notre Dame Cathedral, and the historic Dong Khoi Street.

Guests may explore the city's colourful culture, engage in shopping, and sample the local food with excellent ease.

8. Exceptional Service: Caravelle Saigon is recognized for its attentive and customized service.

The attentive team goes the additional mile to ensure that every guest's requirements are satisfied, giving help with arrangements, and suggestions, and guaranteeing a flawless and pleasurable stay.

9. Meetings & Events amenities: The hotel provides diverse event rooms and state-of-the-art amenities for holding meetings, conferences, weddings, and other special events.

The experienced events team is ready to help in designing and executing unforgettable events with accuracy and attention to detail.

3.2.4 Hotel Majestic Saigon

Hotel Majestic Saigon is a historic five-star hotel situated in the centre of Ho Chi Minh City (Saigon), Vietnam.

With its colonial charm, timeless elegance, and beautiful views of the Saigon River, the hotel provides a sumptuous and unique experience for discriminating tourists.

Here are some important characteristics and attractions of Hotel Majestic Saigon:

1. Colonial Architecture and Tradition: Hotel Majestic Saigon is built in a renovated colonial edifice, reflecting its rich tradition and architectural splendour. The hotel perfectly mixes historic French colonial decor with contemporary conveniences, providing a distinctive and timeless ambience.

2. Spacious Accommodations: The hotel provides a selection of spacious rooms and suites that are attractively designed and well-appointed.

Each room features a harmonious blend of colonial charm and contemporary comfort, with amenities such as plush bedding, marble bathrooms, and panoramic views of the city or the Saigon River.

3. Dining Experiences: Hotel Majestic Saigon features a range of dining alternatives that highlight culinary brilliance.

The Cyclo Café offers a blend of international and Vietnamese dishes in a casual setting, while Serenade Restaurant serves exquisite European cuisine.

Breeze Sky Bar gives a rooftop experience with panoramic views, cool beverages, and live music.

4. Rooftop Pool and Bar: The hotel's rooftop pool is a tranquil oasis where guests can relax and enjoy panoramic views of the city and the Saigon River.

The adjacent Breeze Sky Bar offers a stylish and vibrant atmosphere, perfect for sipping cocktails and enjoying the beautiful sunset.

5. Serene Spa & Wellness: The Spa at Hotel Majestic Saigon provides a selection of revitalizing treatments and therapies to delight and pamper visitors.

From traditional Vietnamese massages to rejuvenating facials, visitors may enjoy relaxation and renewal in a calm and tranquil atmosphere.

6. Central position: Situated in District 1, Hotel Majestic Saigon has a prominent position with easy access to major sights such as the Opera House, Ben Thanh Market, and the historic Dong Khoi Street.

Guests may explore the colourful city, see cultural attractions, and engage in shopping and culinary pleasures.

7. Exceptional Service: Hotel Majestic Saigon is recognized for its attentive and customized service. The committed team works to deliver warm hospitality, ensuring that visitors' requirements are satisfied and their stay is pleasant.

8. Meetings & Events amenities: The hotel provides flexible event rooms and sophisticated amenities for holding meetings, seminars, weddings, and other special events.

The professional events team is available to assist in planning and executing successful and memorable events.

3.2.5 Sheraton Saigon Hotel & Towers

Sheraton Saigon Hotel & Towers is a prominent five-star hotel situated in the centre of Ho Chi Minh City (Saigon), Vietnam.

With its contemporary architecture, great facilities, and friendly hospitality, the hotel delivers a pleasant and memorable experience for discriminating tourists.

Here are some important characteristics and attractions of Sheraton Saigon Hotel & Towers:

1. Contemporary and Stylish Accommodations: The hotel provides large and well-appointed rooms and suites constructed with contemporary elegance and comfort in mind.

Each room includes contemporary conveniences, luxurious bedding, and huge windows that give city views, providing a restful and delightful stay.

2. Dining Experiences: Sheraton Saigon Hotel & Towers has a selection of dining alternatives to please every appetite. Li Bai Restaurant delivers classic Cantonese food in a refined atmosphere, while Saigon Café offers a dynamic buffet with worldwide specialities.

Guests may also enjoy light nibbles and refreshments at the Mojo Bar or a refreshing swim-up bar experience at the Poolside Bar.

3. Resort-like Pool and Fitness Facilities: The hotel offers a tropical outdoor pool surrounded by lush flora, giving a calm getaway from the city's hustle and bustle.

The fitness facility is completely equipped with state-of-the-art equipment, enabling visitors to keep their exercise program throughout their stay.

4. Club Lounge: Sheraton Saigon Hotel & Towers provides an exclusive Club Lounge for guests staying in Club rooms or suites.

The lounge offers a private room where guests may enjoy free breakfast, afternoon tea, and evening drinks, along with customized services and extra amenities.

5. Relaxation at the Spa: The hotel's Aqua Day Spa provides a selection of rejuvenating treatments and therapies aimed to boost relaxation and well-being.

Guests may luxuriate in massages, facials, and body treatments offered by experienced therapists in a calm and peaceful setting.

6. Central position: Situated in District 1, Sheraton Saigon Hotel & Towers boasts a prominent position with easy access to major sights such as the Opera House, Ben Thanh Market, and the historic Dong Khoi Street.

Guests may explore the city's colourful culture, see sites, and enjoy the local food with excellent ease.

7. Meetings & Events amenities: The hotel offers diverse event rooms and sophisticated amenities for holding conferences, weddings, and other special events.

The experienced events team is ready to help in organizing and executing successful and memorable events, guaranteeing a smooth and pleasurable experience for all guests.

8. Warm and Attentive Service: Sheraton Saigon Hotel & Towers is noted for its warm and attentive service.

The devoted team is committed to ensuring that every guest's requirements are satisfied, giving help, advice, and customized attention to ensure a pleasant and memorable stay.

3.3 Top Hotels for Tourists in Da Nang City

3.3.1 InterContinental Danang Sun Peninsula Resort

The InterContinental Danang Sun Peninsula Resort is a luxurious beachside resort situated in Danang, Vietnam. It is located on the Son Tra Peninsula, overlooking the East Sea. The resort is noted for its spectacular vistas, isolated setting, and world-class facilities.

Here are some major characteristics and facts about the InterContinental Danang Sun Peninsula Resort:

1. Lodging: The resort provides a range of lodging choices, including bedrooms, suites, and villas. Each room is created with contemporary Vietnamese elements and provides modern facilities such as flat-screen TVs, spacious bathrooms, and private balconies or patios.

2. Eating: The resort features many eating choices, including restaurants, pubs, and lounges. These places provide a diversity of cuisines, from Vietnamese and Asian delicacies to international and Mediterranean meals.

Guests may enjoy a diversified gastronomic experience while taking in spectacular views of the ocean or neighbouring countryside.

3. Amenities: The InterContinental Danang Sun Peninsula Resort offers a broad choice of amenities for visitors to enjoy.

These include a huge outdoor swimming pool, a fitness centre, a spa providing different treatments, and a private beach area.

There are additional amenities for leisure activities such as tennis, water sports, and hiking.

4. Meetings & Events: The resort provides outstanding settings for meetings, seminars, and special events. It features huge event rooms equipped with the latest technology and can handle both small and large groups.

The resort's gorgeous setting also makes it a popular destination for weddings and other gatherings.

5. Location & Surroundings: The InterContinental Danang Sun Peninsula Resort is located in a beautiful tropical environment, surrounded by the pristine Son Tra Peninsula.

The resort gives tourists convenient access to the neighbouring attractions, including the Marble Mountains, Hoi An Ancient Town, and Ba Na Hills. Danang

International Airport is roughly a 30-minute drive away.

3.3.2 Fusion Maia Da Nang

Fusion Maia Da Nang is a five-star seaside resort situated in Da Nang, Vietnam. It is recognized for its unique idea of wellness and all-inclusive spa treatments.

The resort promises to give a complete experience where visitors may rest, revitalize, and indulge in exquisite treatments.

Here are some major characteristics and facts about Fusion Maia Da Nang:

1. All-Inclusive Spa and Wellness: The resort's distinguishing feature is its all-inclusive spa concept. Every visitor is

entitled to two free spa treatments each day, which may be personalized according to individual tastes.

The spa menu provides a broad selection of services, including massages, facials, body cleanses, and more. The focus is on comprehensive well-being and relaxation.

2. Accommodation: Fusion Maia Da Nang provides large and contemporary villas with private pools or direct access to a community pool.

Each villa has a modern design, opulent facilities, and outdoor living areas. The resort attempts to create a calm and tranquil atmosphere for guests.

3. Eating: The resort provides several eating choices that emphasize healthy and organic food.

The primary restaurant, Five Dining Room, features international and Vietnamese meals produced using locally sourced ingredients. There are additional alternatives for poolside dining, in-villa dining, and private dining experiences.

4. Wellness amenities: In addition to the spa, Fusion Maia Da Nang features various wellness amenities for visitors to enjoy.

These include a fully equipped fitness facility, yoga and meditation courses, a steam room, and a sauna. The resort also provides free health activities such as tai chi and wellness consultations.

5. Location and Surroundings: Fusion Maia Da Nang is situated on My Khe Beach, which is noted for its immaculate white sand and blue seas.

The resort provides spectacular ocean views and is ideally positioned near renowned sights like the Marble Mountains and Hoi An Ancient Town. Da Nang International Airport is roughly a 20-minute drive away.

6. Tailored Experiences: The resort seeks to create individualized experiences for guests. They provide a range of activities and excursions, including cultural tours, culinary workshops, and water sports.

Guests may also personalize their stay with extra spa treatments or specialized wellness programs.

3.3.3 Vinpearl Luxury Da Nang

Vinpearl Luxury Da Nang is a premium five-star resort situated in Da Nang, Vietnam.

It is part of the Vinpearl brand of resorts and is recognized for its lavish rooms, stunning beachfront setting, and comprehensive variety of amenities and services.

Here are some major characteristics and facts about Vinpearl Luxury Da Nang:

1. Accommodation: The resort provides big and attractive bedrooms and suites with contemporary facilities and stylish designs.

Each accommodation is intended to give optimum comfort and has excellent views of either the ocean or the surrounding surroundings. The apartments are furnished with facilities such as flat-screen TVs, minibars, and beautiful bathrooms.

2. Dining: Vinpearl Luxury Da Nang has a range of dining alternatives to suit diverse preferences.

The resort has various restaurants and bars providing a variety of cuisines, including Vietnamese, Asian, and international food. Guests may enjoy exquisite dining experiences and indulge in premium wines and beverages.

3. Facilities and Activities: The resort has a broad choice of facilities and activities to keep visitors amused. It provides a huge swimming pool, a fitness facility, a spa, and a private beach area.

Guests may also enjoy water sports, tennis, and golf at the neighbouring Vinpearl Golf Nam Hoi An. Additionally, the resort includes a Kids Club with activities and amenities for children.

4. Spa & Wellness: The Vincharm Spa at Vinpearl Luxury Da Nang provides a full selection of spa and wellness treatments.

Guests may enjoy numerous treatments, including massages, facials, body cleanses, and traditional Vietnamese remedies. The spa seeks to promote relaxation, regeneration, and a feeling of well-being.

5. Location & Surroundings: The resort is situated on Non-Nuoc Beach, one of the most stunning beaches in Da Nang.

It provides spectacular views of the ocean and is near attractions such as the Marble Mountains and Hoi An Ancient Town. Da Nang International Airport is roughly a 20-minute drive away.

6. Events & Meetings: Vinpearl Luxury Da Nang offers event rooms and services for meetings, conferences, weddings, and other special events.

The resort offers ballrooms and event rooms equipped with the latest technology and can accommodate both small and big parties.

3.3.4 Furama Resort Danang

Furama Resort Danang is a five-star seaside resort situated in Da Nang, Vietnam.

It is one of the most well-established and known resorts in the region, providing beautiful lodgings, large amenities, and a selection of culinary options.

Here are some essential characteristics and facts about Furama Resort Danang:

1. Accommodation: The resort provides a range of accommodation types, including bedrooms, suites, and villas.

The apartments are attractively furnished with contemporary conveniences and offer balconies or patios. Guests may enjoy views of either the ocean or the gorgeous grounds around the property.

2. Dining: Furama Resort Danang is noted for its extensive gastronomic choices. The resort has various restaurants and bars, each giving a distinct eating experience.

Guests may delight in Vietnamese delicacies, international cuisine, seafood meals, and more. There are also possibilities for poolside meals and romantic seaside dinners.

3. Amenities: The resort offers an assortment of amenities to improve visitors' stay. It contains a huge outdoor swimming pool, a workout centre, tennis courts, and a spa.

The spa provides a variety of services, including massages, facials, and body therapies, to encourage relaxation and regeneration.

4. Beachfront position: Furama Resort Danang offers a superb position along the gorgeous Bac My An Beach. Guests get immediate access to the gorgeous white dunes and brilliant turquoise seas.

The resort offers loungers and umbrellas for visitors to relax and soak up the sun. Water sports activities such as kayaking and windsurfing are also accessible.

5. Events & Meetings: The resort provides outstanding settings for weddings, conferences, and other special events.

It features huge ballrooms and function rooms equipped with current technology and can host both small meetings and large-scale events. The resort's stunning surroundings offer a spectacular setting for parties.

6. Nearby Attractions: Furama Resort Danang is conveniently positioned near major attractions.

The UNESCO World Heritage Site of Hoi An Ancient Town is within easy reach, as are the Marble Mountains and the Son Tra Peninsula. Da Nang International Airport is roughly a 15-minute drive away.

3.3.5 Naman Retreat

Naman Retreat is a luxurious seaside resort situated in Da Nang, Vietnam. It is noted for its modern style, serene environment, and holistic health options.

The resort seeks to offer a calm and relaxing environment for guests.

Here are some major characteristics and facts about Naman Retreat:

1. Accommodation: Naman Retreat provides a choice of lodgings, including villas and bedrooms.

The rooms are created with a minimalist and contemporary style, including natural materials and relaxing colour choices. Each apartment is fitted with contemporary conveniences and provides either garden or ocean views.

2. Eating: The resort provides several eating choices that offer a range of cuisines.

The Hay Hay Restaurant delivers a range of foreign specialities, while B Lounge offers a beachside location with magnificent ocean views and a menu of light nibbles and refreshing beverages. The resort also provides in-room meals and exclusive dining experiences.

3. Wellness and Spa: Naman Retreat is recognized for its wellness offers. The resort's spa focuses on traditional Asian medicines and holistic treatments.

Guests may enjoy massages, facials, body cleanses, and other health routines.

The spa also provides yoga and meditation courses, as well as a wellness concierge to help visitors in building individualized health programs.

4. Amenities: The resort has a multitude of amenities to improve visitors' experience. These include various swimming pools, a well-equipped exercise facility, a library, and a beach club.

The resort also includes a Kids Club with activities and amenities for youngsters.

5. Location & Surroundings: Naman Retreat is located on the white sands of Non-Nuoc Beach, only a short drive from

both Da Nang and Hoi An. The resort boasts a calm and private setting, surrounded by beautiful tropical plants. Da Nang International Airport is roughly a 20-minute drive away.

6. Eco-Friendly Design: Naman Retreat is devoted to sustainability and eco-friendly methods. The resort's architecture includes natural features and employs sustainable materials.

It also adopts energy-saving measures and has programs in place to reduce its environmental effect.

3.4 Top Hotels for Tourists in Nha Trang

3.4.1 Six Senses Ninh Van Bay

Six Senses Ninh Van Bay is an outstanding luxury resort nestled on a quiet peninsula in Nha Trang, Vietnam.

Known for its magnificent natural settings, superb service, and dedication to sustainability, the resort provides a genuinely unique and memorable experience for discriminating tourists.

Here are some main elements and attractions of Six Senses Ninh Van Bay:

1. Private Villas with Spectacular Views: The resort has big and tastefully constructed villas that give stunning views of the ocean and the surrounding green countryside.

Guests may pick from a choice of villas, including hilltop villas, beachfront villas, and rock pool villas, each giving solitude, comfort, and lavish facilities.

2. Sustainability and Eco-Friendly Practices: Six Senses Ninh Van Bay is devoted to sustainability and eco-friendly practices.

The resort actively works towards reducing its environmental effect via activities such as trash management, energy saving, and ethical procurement of products.

Guests may enjoy a stay that seamlessly interacts with nature while supporting sustainable tourism.

3. Unspoiled Natural Beauty: The resort is set among spectacular natural beauty, surrounded by pristine beaches, towering mountains, and lush tropical woods.

Guests may explore the area's natural beauties, go climbing in the adjacent mountains, or just rest on the beach and take in the tranquil surroundings.

4. Trademark activities: Six Senses Ninh Van Bay provides a choice of trademark activities that enable visitors to immerse themselves in the local culture and natural beauty.

These adventures may include snorkelling or diving in vivid coral reefs, touring local fishing towns, or going on a sunset cruise.

The resort's devoted crew can construct bespoke itineraries to create amazing experiences.

5. Award-Winning Spa & Wellness: The resort's Six Senses Spa provides a refuge of solitude and refreshment. Guests may enjoy a range of health treatments inspired by Asian traditions, as well as yoga and meditation workshops.

The spa is placed in a quiet location, enabling clients to relax and replenish their minds, body, and soul.

6. Gourmet Eating: Six Senses Ninh Van Bay features a selection of eating alternatives that appeal to varied tastes and preferences.

Guests may have a romantic meal on the beach, eat in the treetop restaurant with panoramic views, or sample foreign and local cuisines at the resort's main restaurant.

The focus is on utilizing fresh, locally sourced ingredients to produce tasty and healthful cuisine.

7. Water and Adventure Sports: The resort provides an assortment of water and adventure sports activities for visitors to enjoy.

From kayaking and paddleboarding to windsurfing and sailing, there are lots of possibilities to explore the surrounding seas.

The resort also offers equipment for snorkelling and scuba diving for people who desire to explore the diverse aquatic life.

8. Wedding and Event Settings: Six Senses Ninh Van Bay offers breathtaking settings for weddings, celebrations, and special events.

9. Personalized Service and Attention to Detail: Six Senses Ninh Van Bay is recognized for its attentive and personalized service.

The resort's specialized personnel goes above and beyond to anticipate and satisfy guests' requirements, guaranteeing a genuinely personalized and unforgettable experience.

3.4.2 Vinpearl Luxury Nha Trang

Vinpearl Luxury Nha Trang is a prominent five-star resort set on its private island, Vinpearl Island, in Nha Trang, Vietnam.

Known for its luxury, world-class facilities, and magnificent beachfront location, the resort delivers a spectacular and unique experience for discriminating tourists.

Here are some main characteristics and attractions of Vinpearl Luxury Nha Trang:

1. Private Island Paradise: Vinpearl Luxury Nha Trang is set on the gorgeous Vinpearl Island, which is accessible by a private cable car or motorboat.

The island features pure white sandy beaches, crystal-clear oceans, and lush tropical scenery, offering a hidden and exclusive getaway for tourists.

2. Luxurious Accommodations: The resort provides stylish and large rooms, suites, and villas that radiate elegance and refinement.

Each room choice is attractively outfitted with contemporary conveniences and provides spectacular views of the ocean or the resort's grounds. Guests may enjoy the maximum luxury and seclusion in their private retreat.

3. World-Class Eating: Vinpearl Luxury Nha Trang provides an assortment of eating alternatives, including various high-end restaurants that appeal to varied gastronomic interests.

From fine dining places selling foreign cuisine to specialized restaurants showcasing Vietnamese specialities, travellers may enjoy a gourmet voyage of tastes and beautiful culinary experiences.

4. Vinpearl Land: As part of the Vinpearl Island complex, visitors have access to Vinpearl Land, a huge amusement park that provides entertainment and thrill for all ages.

The park contains exciting coasters, water slides, an aquarium, a retail centre, and different attractions, offering unending fun and adventure.

5. Vinpearl Golf: Golf lovers may enjoy a game of golf at Vinpearl Golf, an 18-hole championship golf course situated on the island. Designed by IMG Worldwide, the course provides beautiful ocean vistas and challenges players of all ability levels.

Guests may tee off in a scenic environment while enjoying top-notch amenities and services.

6. Luxurious Spa & Wellness Facilities: Vinpearl Luxury Nha Trang features a state-of-the-art spa that provides a broad choice of revitalizing treatments and therapies.

Guests may enjoy relaxing massages, beauty rituals, and holistic wellness experiences that are meant to soothe, energize, and restore balance to the mind and body.

7. Water Sports and Recreation: The resort offers an assortment of water sports and recreational activities for visitors to enjoy.

From snorkelling and diving to jet skiing and parasailing, there are lots of possibilities to explore the diverse marine life and indulge in exhilarating aquatic sports.

The resort also has swimming pools, a fitness centre, and tennis courts for other leisure interests.

8. Wedding & Event Locations: Vinpearl Luxury Nha Trang provides gorgeous locations and great services for weddings, celebrations, and corporate parties.

The resort's specialized event planning staff guarantees that every celebration is expertly prepared and personalized to fit the individual requirements and aspirations of visitors.

9. Impeccable Service and Welcome: Vinpearl Luxury Nha Trang is famous for its superb service and welcoming welcome.

The committed team goes above and beyond to ensure that guests' requirements are fulfilled with the greatest care and attention to detail, delivering a unique and customized experience for each visitor.

3.4.3 Mia Resort Nha Trang

Mia Resort Nha Trang is a boutique beachside resort situated in the gorgeous coastal city of Nha Trang, Vietnam.

Situated on the foothills of the Nha Trang Mountains, the resort provides a calm and personal hideaway with stunning views of the East Sea.

Here are some important characteristics and attractions of Mia Resort Nha Trang:

1. Serene Beachfront Setting: Mia Resort Nha Trang is set on a quiet stretch of Bai Dong Beach, giving guests a serene and intimate beachfront experience.

The resort's position provides amazing panoramic views of the ocean and surrounding natural beauties, providing a calm and tranquil ambience.

2. Excellent Lodgings: The resort provides a selection of excellent lodgings, including villas and rooms, constructed with a modern and minimalist style.

Each lodging choice is well-appointed with contemporary conveniences, private patios or balconies, and large interiors, guaranteeing a pleasant and elegant stay.

3. Individual Service and Attention to Detail: Mia Resort Nha Trang prides itself on offering individual service and attention to detail.

The professional and pleasant staff goes above and beyond to accommodate guests' requirements, delivering a warm and welcoming ambience during their stay.

4. Gastronomic Delights: The resort includes two outstanding dining locations that provide a combination of foreign and Vietnamese cuisines.

Sandals, the seaside restaurant, provides fresh seafood, grilled delicacies, and a range of foreign meals. La Baia, the resort's premier restaurant, provides a sophisticated dining experience with an emphasis on Mediterranean cuisine and beautiful wines.

5. Serene Spa & Wellness: The Xanh Spa at Mia Resort Nha Trang is a haven of relaxation and regeneration.

Guests may luxuriate in a choice of treatments inspired by local traditions, employing natural substances and methods to promote well-being and harmony. The spa also has a steam room and a Jacuzzi for enhanced relaxation.

6. Infinity Pool and Beach Activities: The resort offers a gorgeous infinity pool that overlooks the ocean, giving an ideal area for visitors to recline and enjoy the panoramic views.

For those seeking beach activities, Mia Resort provides kayaking, paddleboarding, and snorkelling, enabling guests to discover the beauty of the surrounding seas.

7. Excursions and Activities: Mia Resort Nha Trang provides numerous excursions and activities to improve visitors' experience.

These may include island hopping, trips to local fishing towns, bike excursions, and culinary courses, allowing the opportunity to learn the local culture, customs, and natural wonders.

8. Wedding & Event Sites: The resort offers stunning sites for weddings, festivities, and special events. Whether it's a modest beach ceremony or a large party overlooking the sea, the resort's event planning staff ensures every detail is precisely prepared to create unforgettable moments.

9. Sustainability Initiatives: Mia Resort Nha Trang is devoted to environmental sustainability. The resort uses eco-friendly techniques such as trash management, energy saving, and assisting local communities.

Guests may enjoy their stay knowing that they are contributing to ethical and sustainable tourism.

3.4.4.Amiana Resort and Villas

Amiana Resort and Villas is a beautiful beachside resort situated in Nha Trang, Vietnam.

Nestled on a secluded cove, the resort provides a tranquil and private refuge for tourists seeking a combination of leisure, natural beauty, and world-class services.

Here are some important characteristics and attractions of Amiana Resort and Villas:

1. Stunning Beachfront Location: Amiana Resort and Villas boast a remarkable location on a private beach, allowing guests direct access to the crystal-clear waters of Nha Trang Bay.

The resort's scenic site affords stunning views of the ocean and neighbouring tropical landscapes, providing a quiet and idyllic ambience.

2. Excellent Accommodations: The resort provides a selection of excellent accommodations, including rooms, suites, and private villas.

Each apartment is attractively designed with contemporary furniture, wide layouts, and private balconies or patios. Guests may enjoy the maximum luxury and solitude while relaxing in the gorgeous natural surroundings.

3. Infinity Pools & Water Features: Amiana Resort and Villas has a variety of gorgeous infinity pools that integrate effortlessly with the surrounding nature.

Guests may take a relaxing plunge in the pools or lounge at the water's edge, enjoying the magnificent views of the harbour.

The resort also has soothing water features and beautiful gardens, contributing to the quiet ambience.

4. Thermo Mineral Pool: One of the distinctive attractions of Amiana Resort and Villas is its Thermo Mineral Pool. The pool is filled with natural hot spring water rich in minerals, allowing visitors a therapeutic and refreshing experience.

Guests may rest in the warm waters, enjoying the therapeutic characteristics of the mineral-rich pool.

5. Gastronomic Delights: The resort provides a range of dining locations that highlight Vietnamese and foreign cuisine.

Bacaro Restaurant provides a choice of Italian-inspired cuisine, while the Pool Bar and the Beach Club serve light nibbles, refreshing drinks, and cocktails.

Guests may experience excellent cuisines in gorgeous surroundings overlooking the bay.

6. Amiana Spa: The Amiana Spa is a sanctuary of calm and relaxation, offering a choice of revitalizing treatments and wellness experiences.

Guests may enjoy relaxing massages, body washes, facials, and holistic treatments utilizing natural and organic materials.

The spa's professional therapists guarantee that customers depart feeling refreshed and energized.

7. Water Sports and Recreational Activities: Amiana Resort and Villas provide a broad choice of water sports and recreational activities for visitors to enjoy.

From kayaking and paddleboarding to snorkelling and diving, there are lots of possibilities to explore the diverse marine life and indulge in exhilarating aquatic experiences.

The resort also has a fitness facility, tennis courts, and yoga courses for people seeking active hobbies.

8. Wedding & Event Settings: The resort offers magnificent settings for weddings, festivities, and special events.

9. Great Service and Welcome: Amiana Resort and Villas are recognized for their great service and friendly welcome.

The courteous and attentive personnel go above and beyond to ensure that visitors' requirements are fulfilled, delivering customized attention and creating a welcome and memorable stay.

3.4.5 InterContinental Nha Trang

InterContinental Nha Trang is a prominent five-star hotel situated in the seaside city of Nha Trang, Vietnam.

With its ideal beachfront location, elegant suites, and world-class services, the hotel delivers a refined and unique experience for discriminating tourists.

Here are some significant characteristics and attractions of InterContinental Nha Trang:

1. Beachfront Location: InterContinental Nha Trang boasts a wonderful location immediately on the beautiful shoreline of Nha Trang Bay.

Guests have easy access to the sandy beach and may enjoy spectacular views of the turquoise ocean and nearby islands, providing a gorgeous and calm location.

2. Magnificent Accommodations: The hotel provides a selection of magnificent rooms and suites that are attractively decorated with contemporary furniture and modern conveniences.

Each lodging choice offers a comfortable and contemporary escape, replete with private balconies giving stunning ocean or city views.

3. Rooftop Infinity Pool: One of the features of InterContinental Nha Trang is its rooftop infinity pool. Situated on the 17th level, the pool provides magnificent views of the harbour and skyline.

Guests may rest in the pool while enjoying the stunning scenery, offering a genuinely unforgettable and sumptuous experience.

4. Spa InterContinental: The hotel boasts a magnificent spa that provides a choice of revitalizing treatments and therapies. Guests may indulge themselves with a choice of massages, facials, and body treatments, meant to encourage relaxation and well-being.

The spa's professional therapists provide a tailored and comprehensive approach to well-being.

5. Gastronomic Delights: InterContinental Nha Trang provides a choice of dining alternatives that appeal to varied gastronomic interests.

Cookbook Cafe delivers an interactive eating experience with live cooking stations and a large buffet dish.

The Lobby Lounge provides a relaxing ambience for afternoon tea, beverages, and light appetizers. Aqualine Bar & Lounge is the ideal venue for refreshing cocktails and spectacular views of the water.

6. Club InterContinental: The hotel's Club InterContinental provides special privileges and tailored services for guests staying in club rooms and suites.

Guests may have access to a private lounge, personal concierge service, free breakfast, afternoon tea, evening drinks, and other premium facilities.

7.   State-of-the-Art   amenities: InterContinental Nha Trang offers a variety of contemporary amenities to improve visitors' experience.

These include a fully equipped fitness facility, a business centre for corporate travellers, and diverse meeting and event rooms for conferences, weddings, and social events.

8. Beach Activities and Water Sports: The hotel provides an assortment of beach activities and water sports for visitors to enjoy.

From sunbathing and swimming to kayaking and jet skiing, there are lots of options to make the most of the gorgeous beachfront setting and partake in exhilarating water sports.

9. Great Service & Hospitality: InterContinental is recognized for its great service and attention to detail, and InterContinental Nha Trang is no exception.

The committed team seeks to surpass guests' expectations by delivering customized and attentive service, assuring a memorable and pleasant stay.

CHAPTER 4

MEANS OF TRANSPORTATION IN VIETNAM

Transportation in Vietnam might be a little tricky for first-time tourists, but with a little bit of planning, it is possible to navigate the country with remarkable ease.

4.1 Getting Around in Cities

Getting about in cities in Vietnam may be an experience in itself, but it is also a chance to explore the nation up close and personal.

Here are some of the most common options for getting around in cities in Vietnam

Motorbikes

Motorbikes are the most common method of transportation in Vietnam's cities, and it's not hard to understand why.

They are speedy, convenient, and simple to park. You may hire a motorcycle at numerous hotels and guesthouses, or from local rental businesses.

Make sure to wear a helmet, and be aware of traffic and road conditions, as motorbike accidents are common in Vietnam.

Bicycles

Bicycles are a popular alternative for moving about in Vietnam's cities, especially for shorter travels. You may hire a bicycle at numerous hotels and guesthouses, or from local rental businesses.

Bicycles are a terrific way to explore the city up close and personal, and they are also excellent exercise.

Walking

Walking is an excellent choice for moving about in Vietnam's cities, especially if you are staying in the city centre.

Walking is free, and it's a terrific opportunity to observe the sights and sounds of the city up close and personal. Be careful of traffic and road conditions, and be sure to wear comfortable shoes.

Public Transportation

Public transportation choices in Vietnam's cities include buses and local railroads. Buses are the most prevalent mode of public transit, with a broad variety of routes and timetables available.

Local trains are also offered in several places, notably in the north.

Taxis and Ride-Sharing Services

Taxis and ride-sharing services like Grab are commonly accessible in Vietnam's cities and may be a handy choice, especially for short travels or if you are not comfortable riding a motorcycle.

Make sure to agree on a price before getting in the taxi, and make sure that the meter is turned on.

If you are utilizing a ride-sharing service like Grab, be careful to validate your driver's identification before getting in the vehicle.

4.2 Intercity Transit in Vietnam

Inter-city transportation in Vietnam is diversified, inexpensive and convenient. Here are some common options for getting around Vietnam between cities

Bus

Buses are the most prevalent and cheap type of inter-city transportation in Vietnam. Several bus companies are providing different sorts of services such as conventional, sleeper, and luxury buses.

The cost of a bus ticket varies based on the distance and kind of service but normally ranges from $5 to $30.

Buses in Vietnam are generally packed, thus it is advisable to book in advance and arrive at the bus terminal early to reserve a seat.

Train

Trains are a pleasant and effective means to travel between places in Vietnam. There are numerous grades of trains available, from basic seats to luxurious cabins with air conditioning.

The railroad network in Vietnam is substantial and links key cities throughout the nation.

The cost of a railway ticket varies based on the distance and class but normally ranges from $10 to $100. It is suggested to buy rail tickets in advance, particularly during the high travel season.

Private Car

Private automobiles or taxis are a handy method to travel between cities in Vietnam, especially for groups or families.

Prices vary based on the distance and the kind of automobile but normally range from $50 to $200.

It is crucial to discuss the fee before commencing the voyage to prevent any misunderstandings. Private automobiles may be obtained via travel firms or Internet booking systems.

Motorcycle

Riding a motorcycle between towns is a popular alternative for daring visitors. It enables you to see the picturesque countryside and stop at numerous sites along the route.

However, it is important to exercise caution and follow local traffic laws. Motorbike rentals are accessible in most major cities in Vietnam, and rates vary from $5 to $20 per day.

4.3 Motorbike rentals

Motorbike rentals are a popular alternative for tourists in Vietnam who wish to explore the country on their own. Here are some things to keep in mind when renting a motorbike in Vietnam

Requirements

To hire a motorcycle in Vietnam, you must have a valid driver's license from your home country or an international driver's license. It is also vital to verify whether your travel insurance covers motorcycle accidents.

Cost

The cost of hiring a motorcycle varies based on the kind of bike, rental period and location. In big cities like Vietnam Hanoi and Ho Chi Minh City, costs normally vary from $5 to $20 per day, whereas in smaller towns and rural regions, rates may be as low as $3 per day.

It is crucial to negotiate the price and check the bike before renting.

Safety

Motorbike accidents are widespread in Vietnam, thus it is crucial to emphasize safety while riding. Always wear a helmet and other safety gear, respect local traffic rules, and drive cautiously.

Be wary of other drivers, particularly in busy places where traffic may be hectic.

Maintenance

Before hiring a motorcycle, examine the bike thoroughly for any damage or concerns. Take note of any existing scrapes or dents, and ensure the brakes, lights, and tires are in excellent shape.

If you detect any difficulties during your rental time, contact the rental agency as soon as possible.

Return

When returning the motorcycle, be sure to return it on time and in the same condition as when you leased it. Take photographs of the bike before and during your rental time to prevent any disagreements about damages.

4.4 Taxis and ride-sharing services

Taxis and ride-sharing services are common forms of transportation in Vietnam, particularly in bigger cities such as Hanoi and Ho Chi Minh City.

Here are some things to keep in mind when using these services

kinds of Services

There are two primary kinds of taxi services in Vietnam - regular taxis and ride-sharing services. Traditional cabs may be hailed on the street or ordered via a taxi company.

Ride-sharing services such as Grab and GoViet are popular options that can be booked using smartphone applications.

Cost

The cost of taxi and ride-sharing services vary based on the distance and time of day. Generally, ride-sharing services are cheaper than regular taxis.

It is vital to clarify the fee with the driver before commencing the journey and to avoid hiring taxis that do not have a meter or set pricing.

Safety

While taxis and ride-sharing services are typically safe in Vietnam, it is crucial to emphasize safety while utilizing them.

Make sure to only use reputable companies, and avoid travelling alone late at night. Always examine the driver's ID, automobile license plate, and make/model before getting in the vehicle.

Payment

Traditional taxis and ride-sharing services normally take cash or credit card payments. It is necessary to discuss the payment option with the driver before commencing the journey.

With ride-sharing services, payment is generally done via the smartphone app, so there is no need to exchange currency with the driver.

Accessibility

Taxis and ride-sharing services are readily accessible in big cities like Hanoi and Ho Chi Minh City but may be less frequent in rural regions. It is a good idea to plan and schedule transportation in advance if you are heading outside of the city.

CHAPTER 5

VIETNAM FOODS AND DRINKS

Vietnamese cuisine is noted for its fresh ingredients, robust tastes, and distinctive cooking methods.

5.1 Vietnamese Cuisine

Vietnamese cuisine is a diversified and tasty cuisine that has been inspired by numerous civilizations throughout its history.

The cuisine's unique balance of nutrients and tastes has made it famous across the globe, and it's now largely regarded as one of the world's healthiest cuisines.

Vietnamese cuisine is distinguished by the use of fresh herbs, vegetables, and meats, as well as the use of numerous spices and sauces.

The tastes in Vietnamese food are frequently a mix of sweet, sour, salty, and spicy. Popular items used in Vietnamese cuisine include rice, noodles, shrimp, chicken, pig, beef, and a range of fresh herbs and vegetables.

One of the most popular meals in Vietnamese cuisine is pho, which is a noodle soup often cooked with beef or chicken broth, rice noodles, and different meats and veggies.

Other popular Vietnamese dishes include banh mi, a sandwich made with a crusty baguette, grilled meat, vegetables, and sauces; banh xeo, a savoury crepe filled with pork, shrimp, and bean sprouts; and goi cuon, fresh spring rolls filled with shrimp, pork, and herbs.

Vietnamese cuisine also features a large range of vegetarian and vegan meals, such as banh mi chay (vegetarian banh mi) and com chay (vegetarian rice dishes).

Some prominent vegetarian components in Vietnamese cuisine include tofu, mushrooms, and other veggies.

Rice is a basic item in Vietnamese cuisine, and it's commonly served with meat or vegetable dishes. Vietnamese rice is frequently aromatic and sticky, and it's sometimes prepared with coconut milk or other flavourings.

Vietnamese cuisine also makes use of a variety of noodles, including rice noodles, egg noodles, and glass noodles. Noodles are utilized in soups, salads, and stir-fry recipes.

One of the primary flavourings of Vietnamese cuisine is nuoc mam, a fish sauce prepared from fermented fish.

Nuoc mam is used in many dishes as a condiment or spice, and it lends Vietnamese cuisine its unique umami taste.

Vietnamese cuisine also makes use of several herbs and spices, including lemongrass, ginger, chilli peppers, and coriander.

Fresh herbs like mint, basil, and cilantro are typically used as garnishes or added to recipes for taste.

Vietnamese food has been inspired by different civilizations throughout the years, including Chinese, French, and Thai cuisines.

These influences have resulted in unique taste combinations and methods that are distinctly Vietnamese.

Vietnamese food is frequently considered healthful owing to its focus on fresh, entire ingredients and balanced tastes.

Many Vietnamese dishes are low in fat and high in protein and fibre, making them a good choice for those looking for nutritious and flavorful meals.

5.2 Street Food

Vietnam is recognized for its colourful street food culture, and experiencing street cuisine is a must-do experience for tourists to the nation.

Here are some key things to know about Vietnamese street food.

Vietnamese street cuisine is often affordable, flavorful, and cooked using fresh ingredients. Street vendors generally specialize in one or two meals, and they frequently have a dedicated following of locals who swear by their cuisine.

Some of the most popular Vietnamese street foods include banh mi (a Vietnamese sandwich filled with meat, vegetables, and condiments), pho (a hearty noodle soup with beef or chicken), bun cha (grilled pork served with rice noodles and herbs), and com tam (broken rice served with various accompaniments).

Street food sellers may be found all around Vietnam, however, some of the greatest street cuisine can be found in areas like Hanoi, Ho Chi Minh City, and Hue.

In Hanoi, for example, the Old Quarter is noted for its small lanes crowded with food shops and sellers.

When eating street food, it's important to choose a vendor that looks clean and busy (indicating that their food is fresh). It's also a good idea to observe the seller prepare the dish to verify that it's cooked fully.

Some street food vendors may not have seating available, so it's common to eat while standing up or sitting on small plastic stools.

This can be a wonderful and engaging experience, as it enables you to mix with people and absorb the bustling vibe of the street.

While street food is generally safe to eat, it's a good idea to exercise caution when trying new dishes.

Some street food may be spicy or have unfamiliar flavours, so it's best to start with small portions and work your way up.

It's also a good idea to remain hydrated and carry a hand sanitiser or wet wipes to clean your hands before eating.

5.3 Traditional Vietnamese Dishes

Vietnamese food is a reflection of the country's geography and history, and it is regarded as one of the healthiest and most flavourful cuisines in the world.

Here are some popular traditional Vietnamese dishes

Pho

This is the most renowned Vietnamese cuisine, and it is created with rice noodles, beef or chicken, and a savoury broth that is cooked for hours with spices like star anise and cinnamon.

It is served with fresh herbs and vegetables such as bean sprouts, basil, and lime.

Banh mi

This is a Vietnamese sandwich constructed with a French baguette, sliced meat (typically pig), pickled veggies, and fresh herbs like cilantro.

Bun cha

This is a popular cuisine in Hanoi, consisting of grilled pig patties served with rice noodles, herbs, and a dipping sauce.

Goi Cuon

These are fresh spring rolls prepared with rice paper, shrimp or pork, and a variety of fresh veggies including lettuce, cucumber, and herbs.

Com tam

This is a dish prepared of broken rice, grilled pork, a fried egg, and other accompaniments such as pickled vegetables and fish sauce.

Bun bo Hue

This is a spicy beef noodle soup that originated in the central area of Vietnam. It is created with a complicated broth that contains lemongrass, shrimp paste, and chile oil.

Ca kho to

This is a dish of braised fish in a caramelized sauce prepared from fish sauce, sugar, and spices like ginger and garlic.

Cha ca

This is a Hanoi delicacy, consisting of turmeric-marinated fish that is pan-fried with dill and served with rice noodles, peanuts, and herbs.

Banh Xeo

A crispy pancake stuffed with pork, shrimp, bean sprouts, and herbs, often served with a sweet and sour dipping sauce.

Mi Quang

A noodle dish originating from the Quang Nam region, comprising yellow noodles, shrimp, pork, herbs, and peanuts in a savoury broth.

Banh Cuon

Steamed rice rolls stuffed with pork and mushrooms, generally served with fried shallots and dipping sauce.

Chao Ga

Rice porridge with chicken and ginger is generally served with a side of crispy fried breadsticks.

5.4 Beverages

Here are some popular Vietnamese beverages

Coffee

Vietnam is noted for its strong and delicious coffee, commonly served with sweetened condensed milk. Some popular varieties include ca phe sua da (iced coffee with condensed milk) and ca phe trung (egg coffee).

Tea

Green tea and jasmine tea are typical alternatives in Vietnam, frequently served hot and unsweetened.

Fruit juice

With a large selection of fresh tropical fruits available, fruit juice is a popular beverage choice in Vietnam. Some common fruits used for juice are passion fruit, mango, and dragon fruit.

Coconut water

Coconut water is a delicious and hydrating beverage in Vietnam, commonly served directly from the coconut with a straw.

Sugarcane juice

Produced from freshly squeezed sugarcane, sugarcane juice is a sweet and pleasant beverage popular in Vietnam.

Herbal beverages

Classic Vietnamese herbal drinks include nuoc sam (ginseng tea) and nuoc mia (sugarcane and ginger juice). These beverages are typically considered to have healing effects.

Rice wine

Rice wine is a powerful alcoholic beverage prepared from fermented glutinous rice, generally offered in tiny glasses as a toast at meals or festivals.

Egg coffee (Cà phê trứng)

A distinctively Vietnamese innovation, this drink is produced by blending egg yolks with sugar and condensed milk, then beating the liquid until it's thick and creamy.

The frothy concoction is then poured over strong Vietnamese coffee, producing a thick and delicious drink.

Sugar cane juice (Nước mía)

Made by crushing sugar cane stalks and extracting juice, this pleasant drink is a popular street snack in Vietnam.

It's normally eaten over ice and may be blended with other fruits like lemon or passionfruit for added taste.

Herbal teas (Trà)

Vietnam has a long history of employing herbs and plants for medical reasons, and many of these herbs are made into teas. Some popular varieties include lotus tea, ginger tea, and lemongrass tea.

Fruit smoothies (Sinh tố)

Made by mixing fresh fruit with ice and condensed milk, these smoothies are a tasty and nutritious way to avoid the heat in Vietnam.

Popular fruits used in sinh tố include mango, banana, papaya, and dragon fruit.

Beer (Bia)

Beer is a popular beverage in Vietnam, with a variety of local brewers manufacturing their kind. Some popular Vietnamese beer

CHAPTER 6

ATTRACTIONS AND CULTURAL SITES ACTIVITIES IN VIETNAM

Attractions and cultural site activities include hiking, caving, and water sports. The nation also provides shopping and market experiences like Ben Thanh Market in Ho Chi Minh City and Hoi An Night Market.

At night, guests may experience the busy nightlife and entertainment scenes on Bui Vien Walking Street, rooftop pubs, and water puppet displays.

6.1 Historical and Cultural Sites

Vietnam is home to several historical and cultural attractions that represent the country's rich past and varied culture.

These sites include historic temples, pagodas, tombs, palaces, museums, and monuments that depict the narrative of Vietnam's history and present.

Some of the most prominent historical and cultural monuments in Vietnam are the Ho Chi Minh Mausoleum, Hue Imperial City, My Son Sanctuary, Cu Chi Tunnels, Temple of Literature, and Hoi An Ancient Town.

6.1.1 Ho Chi Minh Mausoleum in Hanoi

The Ho Chi Minh Mausoleum is a historical and cultural attraction situated in Hanoi, Vietnam. It is the ultimate resting place of Vietnamese revolutionary leader Ho Chi Minh, who was the first President of Vietnam.

The building of the Mausoleum started in 1973 and was finished in 1975.

The architecture of the building was influenced by Lenin's Mausoleum in Moscow, with a grey granite façade and a basic, but powerful, structure. It measures 70 feet tall and is made up of three layers.

Visitors may visit the Mausoleum to pay their respects to Ho Chi Minh. The corpse of Ho Chi Minh is embalmed and sits in a glass cabinet, which is encircled by guards.

Visitors are obliged to dress modestly and politely and must observe a stringent code of behaviour while within the Mausoleum. Cameras and phones are not allowed inside, and visitors are not able to talk or raise their hands while in the building.

The Ho Chi Minh Mausoleum is a prominent symbol of the Vietnamese people's devotion to Ho Chi Minh, who spearheaded the country's war for independence from French colonialism.

The Mausoleum is surrounded by lovely gardens and is next to the Presidential Palace and the One Pillar Pagoda, making it a popular destination for travellers visiting Hanoi.

6.1.2 Hue Imperial City

Hue Imperial City, often known as the Citadel, is a historical and cultural monument situated in the city of Hue, Vietnam.

It was the imperial capital of Vietnam under the Nguyen Dynasty, which reigned from 1802 until 1945.

The building of Hue Imperial City started in 1804 and was finished in 1833. The Citadel has a square design, encircled by walls and a moat. The walls are composed of brick and are 6 meters high, while the moat is 30 meters wide.

The Citadel encompasses an area of roughly 520 hectares and is separated into many parts, including the Imperial Enclosure, the Forbidden Purple City, and the Outer Enclosure.

The Imperial Enclosure is the core area of Hue Imperial City and includes the most notable monuments, including the Thai Hoa Palace, the Hall of Supreme Harmony, and the Nine Dynastic Urns.

The Forbidden Purple City was the private palace of the Nguyen Emperors and was exclusively available to the monarch, his family, and close advisers.

The Outer Enclosure housed the imperial troops, and its architecture was meant to represent the military role of the territory.

Hue Imperial City is a UNESCO World Heritage Site and is regarded as one of Vietnam's most famous sites.

It is a monument to the country's rich cultural legacy and is a popular location for travellers who wish to learn more about Vietnam's imperial past.

Visitors may take a guided tour of the Citadel and see the different monuments, temples, and gardens that make up the complex.

6.1.3 My Son Sanctuary in Hoi An

My Son Sanctuary is a historical and cultural landmark situated in the Quang Nam province of Vietnam, roughly 40 kilometres southwest of Hoi An.

It is a cluster of Hindu temples and towers that were erected between the 4th and 14th centuries by the Champa civilization.

The Champa civilization was a group of autonomous city-states that thrived in what is now central and southern Vietnam from the 2nd to the 17th century.

The temples at My Son were erected as a devotion to the Hindu gods and were a significant focus of the Cham civilisation.

The complex encompasses an area of roughly 142 hectares and is split into 10 groups of buildings. The structures are composed of brick and stone and are embellished with beautiful carvings and sculptures.

The most noteworthy building at My Son Sanctuary is Tower K, which rises 24 meters tall and is regarded as one of the most well-preserved structures at the site.

The temples of My Son Sanctuary were substantially damaged during the Vietnam War but were eventually repaired and awarded a UNESCO World Heritage Site in 1999. The repair work was carried out by the Polish government, and the site is currently preserved by the Vietnamese government.

Visitors to My Son Sanctuary may enjoy a guided tour of the site and learn about the Champa civilization and its religious beliefs.

The temples and towers are surrounded by beautiful green woodlands and are a wonderful example of the old architecture and design of Vietnam.

6.1.4 Cu Chi Tunnels in Ho Chi Minh City

Cu Chi Tunnels is a historical and cultural landmark situated approximately 40 kilometres northwest of Ho Chi Minh City in Vietnam.

It is a network of subterranean tunnels that were utilized by the Viet Cong during the Vietnam War as a base of operations against the South Vietnamese and American troops.

The tunnels encompass an area of around 250 kilometres and consist of a complicated system of subterranean corridors, living quarters, kitchens, storage facilities, and hospitals.

The tunnels were first created by the Viet Minh during the French colonial era but were subsequently developed and modified by the Viet Cong during the Vietnam War.

The tunnels were a key aspect of the Viet Cong's tactics, enabling them to conduct surprise strikes against the enemy and elude notice.

The tunnels were also utilized to transfer supplies and weapons and to offer a haven for the Viet Cong troops and their families.

Today, the Cu Chi Tunnels are a popular tourist attraction in Vietnam, offering visitors a glimpse into the country's wartime past.

Visitors may visit a segment of the tunnel system and learn about the everyday lives of the Viet Cong troops that resided inside. The tunnels are tiny and uncomfortable, and visitors must crawl through certain portions.

In addition to the tunnels, visitors to Cu Chi can also observe a variety of weaponry and traps employed by the Viet Cong throughout the war, including landmines, booby traps, and anti-tank weapons.

There is also a shooting range where visitors can fire a variety of weapons, including AK-47s.

6.1.5 Temple of Literature in Hanoi

The Temple of Literature, also known as Van Mieu-Quoc Tu Giam, is a historical and cultural monument situated in the middle of Hanoi, the capital city of Vietnam.

It was established in 1070 under the reign of Emperor Ly Thanh Tong as a Confucian temple and was also Vietnam's first national university.

The temple is devoted to Confucius, the Chinese philosopher and educator, and celebrates the intellectuals and literary achievements of Vietnam. The temple complex comprises five courtyards, each with its distinctive characteristics and buildings.

The first courtyard, known as the Great Portico, has a massive gate with two tall pillars, known as the Gate of Great Ceremony.

It connects to the second courtyard, which holds the Well of Heavenly Clarity, where students would gather to bathe before taking their examinations.

The third courtyard, known as the Sage Courtyard, includes the primary altar dedicated to Confucius and his four closest students.

The fourth courtyard, known as the Successive Dynasties Courtyard, includes 82 stelae, each sitting on the back of a turtle and etched with the names of Vietnam's most renowned intellectuals.

The fifth and final courtyard, known as the Thai Hoc Courtyard, was the home of

Vietnam's first national university. It was created in 1076 and lasted in operation until 1779, providing courses in Confucianism, literature, and history.

Today, the Temple of Literature is a popular tourist attraction in Hanoi and an important cultural site in Vietnam. It is a testimony to Vietnam's rich cultural legacy and a symbol of the country's devotion to education and research.

Visitors may visit the temple complex and learn about Vietnam's literary and intellectual heritage.

The temple also holds different cultural events and ceremonies throughout the year, including the Vietnamese New Year and the graduation ceremonies for Hanoi's institutions.

The Temple of Literature is a must-visit place for anybody interested in Vietnam's history and culture.

6.2 Natural Wonders & Scenic Spots

Vietnam is home to a multitude of natural treasures and picturesque sites, including Halong Bay, Phong Nha-Ke Bang National Park, Sapa, Ninh Binh, and the Mekong Delta.

Halong Bay, with its beautiful limestone structures, is one of the most famous tourist sites in Vietnam. Phong Nha-Ke Bang National Park is noted for its magnificent cave systems, including the world's biggest cave.

Sapa is a lovely mountain town that provides breathtaking views of terraced rice fields and the surrounding mountains. Ninh Binh is famed for its limestone cliffs, paddy farms, and medieval temples.

The Mekong Delta is a large network of rivers, wetlands, and islands, noted for its floating marketplaces, rice terraces, and fishing settlements.

Whether you're searching for adventure, leisure, or beautiful views, Vietnam's natural treasures and picturesque sites provide something for everyone

6.2.1 Halong Bay

Halong Bay, situated in northern Vietnam, is a natural beauty and one of the country's major tourist sites.

The bay is noted for its green seas, hundreds of towering limestone islands and islets, and stunning natural beauty.

Bay's natural treasures and picturesque spots

Limestone Islands & Islets

Halong Bay is famed for its hundreds of limestone islands and islets that rise spectacularly from the green seas.

These formations are a product of millions of years of geological development and erosion. Some of the most popular islands to visit are Cat Ba Island, Ti Top Island, and Dau Be Island.

Caverns and Grottoes

Halong Bay is home to various caverns and grottoes that are worth investigating. Some of the more popular ones are Thien Cung Cave, Sung Sot Cave, and Trinh Nu Cave.

These caverns include spectacular natural structures such as stalactites, stalagmites, and subterranean lakes.

Floating towns

Halong Bay is also home to many floating towns, where residents live on boats and buildings constructed on stilts. These settlements give a unique glimpse into the everyday life of the residents and their fishing traditions.

Some of the most popular floating villages to visit are Cua Van Floating Village and Vung Vieng Floating Village.

Beaches

Halong Bay offers numerous magnificent beaches, where tourists may rest and enjoy the sun and the water. Some of the most popular beaches are Bai Chay Beach, Tuan Chau Island Beach, and Soi Sim Beach.

Wildlife

Halong Bay is home to various unique and endangered animals, including the Cat Ba Langur, a severely endangered type of monkey found on Cat Ba Island.

Visitors may join eco-tours and explore the bay's natural ecosystems, including coral reefs, mangrove forests, and lagoons.

Sunset and Sunrise

One of the most spectacular vistas in Halong Bay is the sunset and sunrise above the limestone structures. Visitors may enjoy a sunset or dawn boat and watch the magnificent hues and reflections on the green seas.

6.2.2 Phong Nha-Ke Bang National Park

Phong Nha-Ke Bang National Park, situated in central Vietnam, is a UNESCO

World Heritage Site and a natural marvel that offers some of the world's most remarkable cave systems, breathtaking landscapes, and rich flora and wildlife.

Here are the natural wonders and scenic spots of Phong Nha-Ke Bang National Park

Caves & Grottoes

The park is home to approximately 300 caves and grottoes, including the world's longest cave system, Son Doong Cave, which is 5.5 miles long and 650 feet broad.

Other popular caves to explore include Phong Nha Cave, Paradise Cave, and Hang En Cave. These caves are noted by their magnificent structures, such as stalactites, stalagmites, and subterranean rivers.

Karst Mountains

Phong Nha-Ke Bang National Park is home to high karst mountains that rise sharply from the verdant vegetation. These mountains are defined by their distinctive geological formations and provide beautiful views from the summit.

Rivers and Waterfalls

The park is also home to various rivers and waterfalls that provide spectacular vistas and opportunities for outdoor activities like swimming, kayaking, and hiking.

The most popular rivers are Son and Chay Rivers, while the most popular waterfalls include Nuoc Mooc and Phong Nha Waterfalls.

Biodiversity

Phong Nha-Ke Bang National Park is home to an extraordinary variety of flora and wildlife, including over 500 kinds of plants, 98 species of animals, and 338 species of birds.

Some of the most iconic animals in the park are the Saola, a critically endangered species of deer, and the Asiatic Black Bear.

Ethnic communities

The park is also home to various ethnic communities, including the Van Kieu and Chut ethnic tribes.

Visitors may learn about their traditions, rituals, and everyday lives and even engage in traditional activities like weaving and farming.

6.2.3 Sapa Rice Terraces

The Sapa Rice Terraces are a natural marvel and picturesque sight found in Sapa, a hilly area in northern Vietnam.

The terraced fields are the product of centuries of agriculture by indigenous ethnic groups, including the Hmong, Dao, and Giay.

Here are the natural wonders and scenic spots of Sapa Rice Terraces

Rice Terraces

The Sapa Rice Terraces are a spectacular example of sustainable agriculture, with tiered fields reaching up the steep mountain slopes. The fields are filled with water during the rainy season and emptied during the dry season to enable the growing of rice.

The terraces produce a beautiful visual impact, with the varied fields reflecting varying colours of green throughout the year.

Mountains and Valleys

The Sapa Rice Terraces are flanked by high mountains and vast valleys, affording beautiful views of the surrounding countryside.

Visitors may stroll across the terraced fields and up the slopes to experience the spectacular panoramic views of the lowlands below.

Waterfalls and Rivers

The area is also home to various waterfalls and rivers, including the Silver Waterfall and Love Waterfall.

These natural beauties give a refreshing respite from the journey and a chance to appreciate the sound of gushing water and cold mist.

Ethnic communities

The Sapa Rice Terraces are also home to various ethnic communities, including the Hmong, Dao, and Giay.

Visitors may learn about the local traditions, customs, and everyday lives of the ethnic communities via homestays, cultural excursions, and handicraft workshops.

6.2.4 Mekong Delta

The Mekong Delta is a region in southern Vietnam that is recognized for its natural beauty and picturesque locations.

Here are the natural wonders and scenic spots of the Mekong Delta

Mekong River

The Mekong River is the lifeline of the Mekong Delta, supplying water for cultivation and transportation for the local inhabitants.

Visitors may take a boat excursion down the river to observe the beauty of the delta and the everyday life of the people who live along its banks.

Floating Markets

The Mekong Delta is famed for its floating markets, where sellers sell fruits, vegetables, and other things from their boats.

Cai Rang and Phong Dien are two of the most prominent floating markets in the area, where tourists may try local specialities and enjoy the distinctive ambience of the market.

Fruit Orchards

The Mekong Delta is also noted for its fruit orchards, where tourists may enjoy a range of tropical fruits, including mangoes, durians, and jackfruits.

Many orchards also offer homestays and farm tours, giving visitors a chance to learn about the cultivation and harvesting of the fruits.

Canals & Waterways

The Mekong Delta is crisscrossed with canals and waterways that provide a unique opportunity to explore the area.

Visitors may take a boat trip or kayak through the canals to explore the beautiful flora, stilt residences, and floating marketplaces of the delta.

Ecological Reserves

The Mekong Delta is home to various ecological reserves, including Tra Su

Cajuput Forest and U Minh Ha National Park.

These reserves offer a home for a variety of bird and animal species, and visitors may explore the woods and marshes on foot or by boat.

6.2.5 Da Lat Flower Fields

Da Lat is a renowned location in Vietnam noted for its magnificent flower fields and natural attractions.

Here are the natural wonders and scenic spots of Da Lat Flower Fields

Flower Fields

Da Lat is famed for its vivid flower fields, which comprise a variety of flowers such as hydrangeas, dahlias, roses, and many more.

The most popular flower fields are situated on the outskirts of the city and are accessible by motorcycle or vehicle.

Xuan Huong Lake

Xuan Huong Lake is a gorgeous lake situated in the middle of Da Lat City, surrounded by pine trees and flower gardens.

Visitors may hire a boat to sail around the lake or stroll along the lake's shores to enjoy the wonderful sights.

Langbiang Mountain

Langbiang Mountain is the tallest mountain in Da Lat, affording amazing panoramic views of the surrounding surroundings. Visitors may trek up the mountain or take a jeep excursion to reach the peak.

Pongour Waterfall

Pongour Waterfall is a magnificent waterfall situated just outside of Da Lat, surrounded by lush foliage and rugged rocks.

Visitors may swim in the pools at the foot of the waterfall or climb along the paths that lead to the summit.

Dalat Cable Car

The Dalat Cable Car is a unique and fascinating way to experience the city and its surroundings. The cable car gives passengers on a picturesque excursion through pine trees, flower gardens, and valleys.

6.3 Adventure and Outdoor Activities

Vietnam is a nation that provides a broad selection of adventure and outdoor activities for tourists searching for an active and fun holiday.

From climbing in the magnificent highlands of Sapa to water sports in the seaside town of Nha Trang, there are various possibilities to discover the country's natural treasures and experience its distinct culture.

Vietnam also features some of the world's top rock climbing and caving venues, such as Cat Ba Island and Phong Nha-Ke Bang National Park.

With skilled instructors and top-notch equipment, tourists may safely enjoy these exhilarating activities while immersing themselves in Vietnam's natural beauty.

6.3.1 Trekking in Sapa

Sapa is a famous destination in Vietnam for adventure and outdoor lovers, notably for hiking.

Here are amazing things to note about Trekking in Sapa

Picturesque Trails

Sapa is home to several picturesque trails that lead tourists through lush green woods, terraced rice terraces, and tiny towns. Popular paths include the Muong Hoa Valley, Fansipan Mountain, and Cat Cat Village.

Hill Tribe communities

Sapa is home to various hill tribe communities, including the Hmong, Red Dao, and Tay tribes. Visitors may travel through these villages to learn about the local cultures and traditions, and even stay overnight in homestays.

Fansipan Mountain

Fansipan Mountain is the highest mountain in Indochina, towering at 3,143 meters. Visitors may take a multi-day hike to reach the peak, travelling through deep woods, rugged terrain, and beautiful vistas.

Waterfalls

Sapa is home to numerous stunning waterfalls, including Silver Waterfall and Love Waterfall. Visitors may climb these waterfalls, enjoy the breathtaking vistas, and even swim in the pools at the foot of the falls.

Cable Car

For those who desire a more leisurely approach to appreciate the spectacular views of Sapa, the Fansipan Legend Cable Car carries tourists from the foot of Fansipan Mountain to the peak, affording amazing panoramic views of the surrounding landscapes.

6.3.2 Water Sports in Nha Trang

Nha Trang is a coastal city situated in the south-central area of Vietnam, and it is noted for its crystal-clear seas and white sandy beaches.

Here are the adventure and outdoor activities of water sports in Nha Trang

Snorkelling

Nha Trang is home to some of the most magnificent coral reefs in Vietnam, making it a fantastic site for snorkelling.

Visitors may hire snorkelling gear or take a snorkelling trip to explore the underwater world and witness a variety of tropical fish and coral.

Scuba Diving

For those who seek a more immersed experience, scuba diving is also a popular water activity in Nha Trang. Various dive facilities provide PADI certification courses and guided dives for all levels of expertise.

Parasailing

Parasailing is an exciting water activity that enables guests to experience panoramic views of Nha Trang's coastline while being pulled by a speedboat. This exercise is suited for all ages and doesn't need any specific skills or expertise.

Jet Skiing

Jet skiing is another popular water activity in Nha Trang that gives a pleasant and thrilling experience.

Visitors may hire a jet ski and ride the waves along the shoreline, admiring the beauty and experiencing the rush of excitement.

Banana Boat Ride

The banana boat ride is a fun-filled activity perfect for families and groups of friends.

The inflatable boat fashioned like a banana is towed by a speedboat, and passengers can hold on tight while they ride the waves.

Kayaking

Kayaking is a terrific way to explore the serene waterways of Nha Trang and find secret coves and private beaches.

Visitors may hire kayaks or join a guided trip to explore the nearby islands and appreciate the spectacular natural surroundings.

6.3.3 Motorbiking through the Hai Van Pass

Motorbiking via the Hai Van Pass is one of the most popular adventures and outdoor sports in Vietnam, situated between the towns of Da Nang and Hue.

Here are the adventure and outdoor activities of motorbiking through the Hai Van Pass

Beautiful route

The Hai Van Pass is a beautiful route that provides amazing views of the coast, mountains, and farmland.

Motorbiking across the pass enables tourists to see the grandeur of Vietnam's environment while feeling the wind in their hair.

Historical Sites

The Hai Van Pass is particularly rich in history since it functioned as a crucial position throughout the Vietnam War. Visitors may stop at the top of the pass to observe the Hai Van Gate, a fortress erected during the Nguyen Dynasty.

Local Culture

Motorbiking across the Hai Van Pass also offers tourists the opportunity to explore the local culture of Vietnam.

Visitors may stop at tiny towns along the journey to mingle with residents, enjoy traditional cuisine, and learn about the country's rich past.

Photography

The Hai Van Pass is a famous site for photography aficionados since it provides amazing panoramic vistas and lovely surroundings.

Visitors may record unforgettable moments and take home unique keepsakes of their journey.

Experience

Motorbiking via the Hai Van Pass is a thrilling experience that delivers a surge of excitement. The twisting roads and steep inclines offer a tough ride for experienced motorcyclists, making it a great pastime for thrill-seekers.

Trip Options

Visitors may opt to motorcycle across the Hai Van Pass on their own or join a guided trip.

Guided tours give the benefit of having a knowledgeable guide who can provide insight into the history and culture of the place

6.3.4 Caving in Phong Nha-Ke Bang National Park

Caving at Phong Nha-Ke Bang National Park is a popular adventure and outdoor activity that allows guests a chance to experience one of the world's most unique and magnificent natural marvels.

Here are the adventure and outdoor activities of caving in Phong Nha-Ke Bang National Park

World-Class caverns

Phong Nha-Ke Bang National Park is home to approximately 300 caverns, several of which are world-class and have been designated as UNESCO World Heritage Sites.

Visitors may explore a variety of caverns, from tiny and basic to huge and complicated, each with its distinct qualities.

Caving excursions

Visitors may take caving excursions that cater to a variety of ability levels, from beginner to experienced.

These excursions are supervised by trained guides who give tourists the required equipment and safety gear, as well as information on the history and geology of the caverns.

Spectacular environment

Caving in Phong Nha-Ke Bang National area offers tourists the opportunity to explore the spectacular natural environment of the area.

The caverns are loaded with magnificent rock formations, subterranean rivers, and gorgeous stalactites and stalagmites, providing for a very unforgettable and unique encounter.

Physical Challenge

Caving in Phong Nha-Ke Bang National Park presents a physical challenge for individuals who appreciate outdoor sports.

Visitors will need to climb, crawl, and manoeuvre through small corridors, making for a thrilling and gratifying experience.

Educational Experience

Caving at Phong Nha-Ke Bang National Park is also an educational experience, as tourists may learn about the geological and historical importance of the caverns.

The park's guides are knowledgeable and give insight into the development and history of the caverns.

Sustainable Tourism

Phong Nha-Ke Bang National Park is devoted to sustainable tourism, which means that visitors may enjoy the park's natural beauty while reducing their influence on the environment.

6.3.5 Rock climbing at Cat Ba Island

Rock climbing on Cat Ba Island is a popular adventure and outdoor sport that allows tourists a chance to see the breathtaking natural beauty of the island while challenging their physical strength and endurance.

Here are the adventure and outdoor activities of rock climbing on Cat Ba Island

Spectacular Scenery

Cat Ba Island is recognized for its spectacular limestone cliffs and rock formations, making it a great location for rock climbing aficionados.

The island's steep topography offers a tough and exciting climbing experience, with panoramic views of the surrounding countryside.

Range of Routes

Cat Ba Island provides a range of climbing routes to suit all ability levels, from novice to experienced. The island boasts around 300 recognized routes, with varied degrees of difficulty and style, making it a fantastic location for climbers of all abilities.

Professional experts

Visitors may join rock climbing trips that are guided by professional experts who offer the essential equipment and safety gear, as well as expert coaching on climbing methods and route selection.

These guides are informed of the island's geology and can give insights into the history and development of the rock formations.

Physical Challenge

Rock climbing at Cat Ba Island is a physically hard exercise that involves strength, endurance, and focus.

Climbers will need to utilize their full body to handle the steep terrain, giving it a fantastic exercise and a chance to challenge one's physical boundaries.

Educational Experience

Rock climbing at Cat Ba Island is also an educational experience, as climbers may learn about the geology and history of the island's limestone cliffs and rock formations.

The island's guides are informed and can give insights into the formation and history of the cliffs.

Sustainable Tourism

Cat Ba Island is devoted to sustainable tourism, which means that tourists may enjoy the island's natural marvels while reducing their influence on the environment. Visitors are urged to obey the island's standards and leave no trace behind.

6.4 Shopping and Markets in Vietnam

Vietnam is renowned for its crowded markets and vivid street scenes, making it a perfect location for those interested in shopping and seeing local culture.

Here are some of the must-visit shopping and market destinations in Vietnam

6.4.1 Ben Thanh Market in Ho Chi Minh City

Ben Thanh Market in Ho Chi Minh City is one of the most renowned marketplaces in Vietnam and a popular destination for residents and visitors alike. The market has been there since the 19th century and is an important icon in the city.

Ben Thanh Market is situated in the middle of the city and is readily accessible by public transit.

The market is a vast area with a variety of vendors offering everything from local handicrafts and souvenirs to fresh fruit and street cuisine.

It's a terrific spot to explore the local culture and immerse yourself in the hustle and bustle of a typical Vietnamese market.

One of the nicest things about Ben Thanh Market is the range of items offered. Visitors may find anything from traditional garments and fabrics to jewellery, artwork, and gadgets.

The market is mainly noted for its food vendors, which serve a broad choice of local foods, snacks, and beverages.

Some of the must-try dishes at Ben Thanh Market include banh mi sandwiches, pho noodle soup, and fresh spring rolls. Visitors may also enjoy local specialities such as durian fruit and Vietnamese coffee.

While shopping at Ben Thanh Market, visitors should be prepared to bargain for prices. Bargaining is a prevalent activity in Vietnamese marketplaces, and tourists may frequently find better discounts by bartering with sellers. It's also crucial to be alert to pickpockets and keep a watch on your valuables.

6.4.2 Dong Xuan Market in Hanoi

Dong Xuan Market in Hanoi is one of the oldest and biggest marketplaces in Vietnam, situated in the centre of the city's Old Quarter.

The market was created in the late 19th century and has been a popular attraction for residents and visitors alike ever since.

Dong Xuan Market is a multi-level complex with approximately 5,000 booths offering a broad variety of commodities, including apparel, textiles, electronics, food, and household items.

Visitors may easily spend hours walking around the market's small lanes and checking out the numerous things on sale.

One of the attractions of Dong Xuan Market is the food department, which is situated on the first level.

Here, tourists may discover a variety of street food booths serving classic Vietnamese meals such as pho noodle soup, banh mi sandwiches, and fresh spring rolls. The market is also an excellent spot to enjoy local specialities such as egg coffee and Hanoi-style pho.

Another distinctive characteristic of Dong Xuan Market is the area devoted to pets and animals. Here, visitors may discover a large choice of birds, fish, turtles, and other creatures for sale, as well as pet supplies and accessories.

Like many Vietnamese marketplaces, bargaining is a typical activity in Dong Xuan Market. Visitors should be prepared to negotiate with merchants to acquire the best deals, and should also be alert to pickpockets and keep their possessions nearby.

6.4.3 Hoi An Night Market

Hoi An Night Market is a renowned shopping and marketplace in Hoi An, a seaside city in central Vietnam. The market is situated in the old town of Hoi An, a UNESCO World Heritage site, and is recognized for its lively and colourful environment.

The market is open every night from 5 pm till late and contains hundreds of sellers offering a broad variety of things.

The night market is notable for its traditional Vietnamese handicrafts, including ceramics, needlework, and lanterns.

Visitors may also discover a variety of street food sellers, dishing up delectable local specialities like Cao Lau noodles and Banh Mi sandwiches.

The market is also a wonderful area to purchase gifts including apparel, purses, and jewellery, as well as distinctive Vietnamese delicacies like coconut sweets and rice paper.

One of the features of the Hoi An Night Market is the lanterns that light up the streets, creating a wonderful ambience.

Visitors may buy their lanterns and throw them into the river, a traditional rite thought to bring good luck

6.4.4 Saigon Square in Ho Chi Minh City

Saigon Square is a prominent retail centre situated in the middle of Ho Chi Minh City (previously known as Saigon), the biggest city in Vietnam.

The market is a busy centre for residents and visitors alike, recognized for its broad range of items and inexpensive rates.

Saigon Square contains numerous floors of stores and vendors offering anything from apparel and shoes to electronics and household items.

Bargaining is a frequent activity at the market, and tourists are urged to bargain with merchants to acquire the best discounts.

The market is notably popular among fashion-conscious residents and tourists since it includes a broad range of stylish apparel and accessories at moderate costs.

Visitors may discover anything from streetwear and sportswear to designer-inspired apparel and accessories.

In addition to apparel, Saigon Square is also an excellent area to buy technology, with stores offering anything from cellphones and computers to cameras and other devices.

Other popular items at the market include handbags, watches, sunglasses, and souvenirs like keychains and magnets.

6.4.5 Hang Gai Street in Hanoi

Hang Gai Street, commonly known as Silk Street, is a prominent shopping attraction situated in the ancient area of Hanoi, Vietnam.

The street is noted for its broad array of silk goods, including clothes, accessories, and home décor items.

Visitors to Hang Gai Street may discover a variety of silk items, from traditional Vietnamese apparel like the ao dai to contemporary clothing designs and accessories.

Many of the shops on the street offer custom tailoring services, allowing visitors to have their custom-made silk garments created on the spot.

In addition to silk goods, Hang Gai Street also displays a range of other traditional Vietnamese artefacts including lacquerware, pottery, and hand-woven fabrics. Visitors may discover unique souvenirs and presents to take home from their vacation to Vietnam.

The street itself is dotted with ancient colonial-style houses and traditional

Vietnamese architecture, creating a lovely and delightful shopping experience. Street vendors and food booths also dot the neighbourhood, providing a choice of local delicacies and drinks.

6.5 Nightlife and Entertainment

Vietnam provides a varied choice of nightlife and entertainment alternatives for travellers.

Here are some of the top attractions in this category

6.5.1 Bui Vien Walking Street in Ho Chi Minh City

Bui Vien Walking Street is situated in the centre of Ho Chi Minh City's District 1, and it is a popular location for both residents and visitors searching for a colourful nighttime experience.

The area is studded with bars, clubs, restaurants, tourist stores, and street vendors offering native delicacies and beverages.

The environment is bright and enthusiastic, with music booming from the bars and people enjoying themselves.

The street comes alive at night and is the ideal spot to get a drink, dance the night away, and take in the colourful vibe of the city. It's also a terrific area to people-watch and absorb the local culture.

6.5.2 Hanoi Opera House

The Hanoi Opera House is a spectacular architectural marvel situated in the middle of Hanoi, the capital city of Vietnam.

Built in 1911 by French architects, the edifice was formerly utilized as a venue of amusement for the French colonialists. Today, it remains an iconic symbol of Hanoi's culture and history.

The Hanoi Opera House includes a neoclassical style with elegant balconies, majestic staircases, and a vast auditorium with a capacity of over 600 seats. The inside is richly furnished with elaborate carvings and chandeliers, creating an aura of elegance and refinement.

The Opera House features a range of events throughout the year, including ballet, classical music, traditional

Vietnamese opera, and contemporary productions.

It is also a famous place for significant national and international events, including conferences, cultural festivals, and diplomatic meetings.

Visitors to the Hanoi Opera House may take a guided tour of the facility to learn more about its history and architecture. The visits include access to the main lobby, the auditorium, and the backstage area.

Alternatively, visitors can purchase tickets to attend one of the many performances held at the Opera House and experience its majestic ambience firsthand.

6.5.3 Rooftop Bars in Ho Chi Minh City

Rooftop bars have been more popular in recent years as one of the greatest ways to experience Ho Chi Minh City's dynamic nightlife. These pubs provide spectacular views of the city's skyline, amazing drinks, and typically a relaxing setting to rest after a hectic day of touring.

Here are some of the top rooftop bars in Ho Chi Minh City

Chill Skybar

Located on the 25th level of the AB Tower, Chill Skybar is one of the most popular rooftop bars in the city.

It provides spectacular views of the city skyline and serves a comprehensive variety of cocktails and other beverages.

The environment is stylish and elegant, and it is a perfect setting for a night out with friends or a romantic evening.

The Rooftop Saigon

Located on the 9th story of the Rex Hotel, The Rooftop Saigon provides panoramic views of the city's cityscape and the Saigon River.

The bar provides a broad choice of beverages, from traditional cocktails to artisan brews. The ambience is pleasant and low back, and it is a favourite destination for both visitors and residents.

Broma

Not as far up as some of the other rooftop bars, Broma is situated on the 18th story of a skyscraper in the centre of the city.

It provides fantastic views of the lively streets below and serves a choice of beverages, including a nice selection of beers. The ambience is vibrant, and it is a favourite destination for both foreigners and locals.

Saigon Saigon Rooftop Bar

Located on the 9th level of the Caravelle Saigon Hotel, the Saigon Saigon Rooftop

Bar is one of the city's oldest and most renowned rooftop bars.

It provides panoramic views of the city and has a classic, refined ambience. It is a terrific setting for a night out with friends or a romantic evening.

Social Club Rooftop Bar

Located on the 23rd story of the Hotel Des Arts Saigon, the Social Club Rooftop Bar is a popular venue with a contemporary and sophisticated environment.

It provides panoramic views of the metropolitan skyline and serves a choice of beverages, including unique cocktails. The pub routinely holds events and parties, making it a popular destination for both visitors and residents.

6.5.4 Nightclubs in Hanoi

Hanoi, the capital of Vietnam, boasts a thriving nightlife scene with a range of nightclubs presenting diverse genres of music and atmospheres.

Whether you love electronic dance music, live music, or a combination of both, you'll find a club that meets your taste.

One of the most famous nightclubs in Hanoi is Savage, which is noted for its techno and house music. The club features a minimalist and industrial décor and is set in a basement, giving a distinct vibe.

Another popular nightclub is Hero Club, which offers a more upmarket and opulent ambience with a mix of electronic and live music.

Dragonfly is another renowned club, situated in the Old Quarter of Hanoi. It boasts a trendy and elegant environment with a mix of electronic dance music and live shows.

If you're looking for a more laid-back ambience, you may go to CAMA ATK, which offers a quiet and intimate feel with live music performances by local and international performers.

6.5.5 Water Puppet Shows in Hanoi

Water puppet performances are a prominent type of traditional entertainment in Vietnam, notably in Hanoi.

The acts are performed in a pool of water, with the puppeteers standing waist-deep behind a screen, controlling the puppets with long poles.

The presentations showcase tales from Vietnamese mythology and history, frequently with live music accompaniment.

The water puppetry tradition goes back to the 11th century in the Red River Delta of northern Vietnam, where people would perform the acts in rice fields during festivals.

Hanoi is the greatest spot to enjoy water puppet shows in Vietnam, with multiple theatres in the city giving daily performances.

The Thang Long Water Puppet Theater is one of the most popular, situated in the centre of the Old Quarter. The concerts are done completely in Vietnamese, yet it is simple to follow along with the graphics and music.

The concerts normally run from 45 minutes to an hour and are suited for all ages. Visitors should reserve tickets in advance to assure availability, particularly during high tourist season.

CHAPTER 7

PROVEN & PRACTICAL TIPS FOR TRAVELING IN VIETNAM

Below are the practical tips for travelling in Vietnam

7.1 Language

The official language of Vietnam is Vietnamese, and while many people speak English, particularly in tourist regions, it's still a good idea to learn some basic Vietnamese phrases before you arrive.

This will assist you to find your way about and converse with people who don't speak English.

Some vital phrases to learn are "xin chào" (hello), "cảm ơn" (thank you), "tạm biệt" (goodbye), and "bạn có nói tiếng Anh không" (do you speak English).

It's also worth mentioning that the Vietnamese language is tonal, meaning that the meaning of a word may alter based on the tone used while pronouncing it.

It might be tough for non-native speakers to grasp, but locals will appreciate your attempts to converse in their language.

7.2 Etiquette and Customs

Vietnamese culture lays a significant emphasis on respect and civility, especially towards elders and those in positions of power.

It is necessary to greet individuals correctly, using their title or honorific and a handshake or bow, and to avoid physical contact that may be deemed improper.

When visiting temples or other religious sites, it is important to dress modestly and remove shoes before entering.

It is also vital to be careful of local customs and traditions, such as removing headwear while entering particular buildings or avoiding pointing with one's foot.

In addition, it is considered disrespectful to raise one's voice or display anger in public, and it is necessary to avoid inflicting loss of face or shame on others.

7.3 Tipping

Tipping is not a prevalent practice in Vietnam and is not anticipated in most circumstances.

However, tipping is becoming more common in tourist areas and upscale establishments.

If you do decide to tip, it's normally recommended to use cash and offer a modest sum, such as 10% of the entire cost or rounding up to the next whole number.

Some restaurants and cafes may include a service charge in the bill, so it's worth checking before leaving an additional tip.

It's crucial to know that tipping might be perceived as a show of disrespect in certain scenarios.

For example, tipping someone in a position of power, such as a police officer or government official, might be perceived as a bribe and is prohibited. It's also not common to tip street sellers or taxi drivers.

If you experience great treatment from a tour guide, driver, or hotel staff member, a modest tip may be appreciated. However, it's always best to check with your tour company or hotel to see if they have any specific guidelines regarding tipping.

7.4 Bargaining

Bargaining is a popular activity in Vietnam, particularly while purchasing at marketplaces or street sellers. It is anticipated that both sides would participate in negotiation until a mutually acceptable price is achieved.

Some tips for negotiating in Vietnam include

i. Start by providing a price that is lower than what you are prepared to spend, but still fair.

ii. Don't be scared to walk away if you can't agree on a price. Often, the vendor will call you back and agree to your offer.

iii. Be pleasant and respectful throughout the negotiation process. Remember that negotiating is a part of Vietnamese culture, and it is not intended to be confrontational or violent.

iv. Take your time and don't hurry the procedure. Enjoy the haggling process and attempt to learn more about the seller and their items.

v. If you're doubtful about a product's quality or authenticity, ask the dealer for further information or a demonstration.

vi. Keep in mind that certain products, such as food and beverages, may not be accessible to negotiate.

7.5 Using Technology and the Internet

Using technology and the internet is becoming more and more crucial for tourists, particularly in Vietnam where cellphones and internet access are popular.

Here are some recommendations for utilizing technology and the Internet in Vietnam

SIM cards

Buying a local SIM card is a quick and economical method to remain connected. You can get SIM cards at the airport or convenience shops, and they normally cost about 100,000 VND (roughly $4) for a week or two of data and calls.

Wi-Fi

Most hotels, restaurants, and cafés in large cities provide free Wi-Fi, however, the quality and speed of the connection might vary. It's usually a good idea to have a backup plan in case the Wi-Fi is not functioning.

Applications

Various applications might be beneficial for tourists in Vietnam. Google Maps is an excellent tool for obtaining directions and locating locations of interest. Grab and GoViet are famous ride-hailing applications that make it simple to move around cities.

Traveloka and Agoda are good for arranging accommodation, while Foody and TripAdvisor can help you locate fantastic places to eat.

Power adapters

Vietnam utilizes 220V power outlets, and the sockets are commonly two-pronged. If you're travelling from a nation with a different voltage or plug type, make sure to carry a power adaptor.

VPNs

Access to various websites and social media platforms may be blocked in Vietnam, so utilizing a VPN might be useful.

A VPN (Virtual Private Network) enables you to surf the internet safely and secretly by routing your connection via a server located elsewhere.

Online scams

Be wary of online fraud while using the internet in Vietnam. Don't give out personal information or pay money to somebody you don't know. Use reputable websites and apps for booking and purchasing items online.

7.6 Staying Safe and Healthy

Staying safe and healthy is an important aspect to consider when travelling in Vietnam.

Here are some practical tips to ensure your safety and well-being during your trip

Health precautions

Make sure you are up to date with basic immunizations before coming to Vietnam. Hepatitis A and typhoid are suggested.

Mosquito-borne illnesses such as dengue fever and malaria are widespread in specific locations of Vietnam, hence it is essential to take steps to minimize mosquito bites.

Also, avoid tap water and ice, and be cautious about consuming raw or undercooked foods.

Traffic safety

Traffic may be hectic and unpredictable in Vietnam, particularly in large cities like Hanoi and Ho Chi Minh City. Be careful while crossing the street and consider hiring a transportation service or renting a motorcycle from a reliable firm. Always wear a helmet while riding a motorcycle.

Frauds

Tourist frauds are frequent in Vietnam, especially in tourist areas. Always be mindful of your surroundings and don't trust people lightly.

Avoid exchanging currencies with street sellers and always utilize reputed money exchange businesses.

Respect local culture

Vietnam has a rich cultural legacy, and it's crucial to be respectful of local customs and traditions.

For example, dress modestly while visiting temples and religious places, take off your shoes when entering someone's house or a temple, and avoid public shows of love.

Emergency services

Make sure you have access to emergency services such as hospitals, police, and fire stations. Keep a list of emergency numbers with you at all times and consider purchasing travel insurance before your trip.

CONCLUSION

Vietnam is an interesting and attractive nation that provides a plethora of experiences to tourists. From its rich history and culture to its gorgeous natural vistas and exquisite food, Vietnam offers something for everyone.

This travel guide has provided a comprehensive overview of the various aspects of travelling to Vietnam, including planning your trip, accommodations, transportation, food and drink, attractions and activities, shopping and markets, nightlife and entertainment, as well as practical tips for staying safe and healthy while exploring the country.

Whether you're searching for an exciting outdoor expedition, a cultural experience, or a calm beach holiday, Vietnam offers it all.

With this book as your companion, you can travel the nation with confidence and optimize your time experiencing everything that it has to offer.

I hope that this book has given you the knowledge and inspiration you need to plan your next trip to Vietnam. Happy travels!

Printed in Great Britain
by Amazon